FROM PRISON GRIEVANCES TO COURT

How to File and Win Guidebook

Sophia J. Quill

Freebird Publishers

221 Pearl St., Ste. 541, North Dighton, MA 02764
Info@FreebirdPublishers.com
www.FreebirdPublishers.com

All Freebird Publishers titles, imprints, and distributed lines are available at special quantity discounts for bulk purchases for sales promotions, premiums, fundraising, educational, or institutional use.

ISBN: 978-1-952159-43-5

Printed in the United States of America

CONTENTS

INTRODUCTION TO ADMINISTRATIVE REMEDY PROGRAM

The Administrative Remedy Program provides every inmate with the opportunity to seek a formal review of a grievance concerning virtually any aspect of his or her confinement, should informal procedures not achieve resolution. See 28 C.F.R. pt. 542, subpart. B: *Administrative Remedy Program*, Program Statement 1330.18. This program applies to all inmates confined in institutions operated by the Bureau of Prisons (BOP), inmates designated to contract Residential Reentry Centers (RRC), and to former inmates for issues that arose during confinement. Inmates are obligated to attempt informal resolution of grievances prior to filing a formal request for administrative remedy. Once a formal request is filed at the institution level ("BP-9"), the Warden of that facility has 20 days to investigate and provide the inmate with a written response. If the inmate is dissatisfied with the Warden's response, he or she has 20 days to file a Regional Administrative Remedy Appeal ("BP-10"). Once received in the Regional Office, the Regional Director has 30 days to investigate and provide the inmate with a written response. If the inmate is dissatisfied with the Regional Director's response, he or she has 30 days to file a Central Office Administrative Remedy Appeal ("BP-11"). Once received in the Central Office, the Administrator, National Inmate Appeals, has 40 days to investigate and provide the inmate with a written response. After receiving the Administrator's response, the inmate has exhausted the BOP's Administrative Remedy Program. The program provides for expedited investigations and responses in emergency situations, as well as providing extensions of time for both filing grievances and receiving responses. No time limit is imposed upon an inmate raising allegations of sexual abuse through the administrative remedy system.

If the inmate considers the issue to be sensitive, e.g., the inmate's safety or well-being would be placed in danger if the request became known at the institution, the inmate may submit the appeal directly to the appropriate Regional Director. The inmate must mark the request as "sensitive" and explain in writing the reason for not submitting the request to the institution. If the Regional Administrative Remedy Coordinator agrees that the request is sensitive, the request shall be accepted and investigated, and a response will be generated. Otherwise, the request will not be accepted, and the inmate shall be advised in writing of that determination without a return of the request. The inmate may then pursue the matter by submitting a request for Administrative Remedy locally to the Warden. The Warden shall allow a reasonable extension of time for such a resubmission.

The PLRA requires prisoners to exhaust administrative remedies before filing a suit in federal court. That statute provides that "[n]o action shall be brought with respect to prison conditions under section 1983 of this title, or any other Federal law, by a prisoner confined in any jail, prison, or other correctional facility until such administrative remedies as are available are exhausted." *See* 42 U.S.C. § 1997e(a). *See also Porter v. Nussle*, 534 U.S. 516 (2002); *Booth v. Churner*, 532 U.S. 731 (2001). Exhaustion is mandatory in *Bivens* actions. However, exhaustion in habeas petitions has been judicially created. Exhaustion is generally expected; however, courts may waive it in cases where they believe exhaustion would have been futile. The requirement to exhaust the administrative remedy process serves to (1) promote administrative efficiency by preventing premature judicial interference with agency processes; (2) encourage respect for executive autonomy by allowing an agency the opportunity to correct its own errors; (3) facilitate judicial review by affording courts the benefits of an agency's experience and expertise; and (4) serve judicial economy by having the agency compile the factual record.

The Supreme Court reaffirmed these holdings mentioned above, in *Woodford v. Ngo*, 548 U.S. 81, 90-91 (2006), and mandated "…compliance with an agency's deadlines and other critical procedural rules because no adjudicative system can function effectively without imposing some orderly structure on the course of its proceedings." The Supreme Court further held in *Woodford*, "[t]he text of 42 U.S.C. § 1997e(a) strongly suggests that PLRA uses the term 'exhaustion' to mean…proper exhaustion." Section 1997e(a) refers to "such administrative remedies as are available" and thus points to the doctrine of exhaustion in administrative law. *See Jones v. Bock*, 549 U.S. 199 (2007).

The BOP Administrative Remedy Program is administered differently for inmates in private facilities. Should an inmate at a private facility wish to appeal a local decision, the inmate may file with the local institution. Inmates in private facilities who wish to grieve a specific BOP matter (which is limited to classification, designation, sentence computation, reduction of

The term "*Bivens* actions" stems from the case *Bivens v. Six Unknown Named Agents of Federal Bureau of Narcotics*, 403 U.S. 388 (1971). In a *Bivens* action, an inmate is suing a staff member in their individual capacity, alleging that the staff member intentionally or maliciously violated an inmate's clearly established constitutional right. The inmate seeks monetary damages directly from the employee, not the U.S. Government, sentence, removal, or disallowance of Good Conduct Time, or issues directly involving BOP staff. may utilize the progressive BOP administrative remedy process available to all federal inmates. The appeal must then be filed with the Chief of the BOP's Privatization Management Branch.

AUTHOR'S INTRODUCTION

This book began as notes I wrote to help myself, and then to assist others in navigating the administrative remedy process.

Every federal or state prison has an administrative remedy or grievance procedure. It's one of the steps you have available to address any violations or wrongs against you. Learning how to use the administrative remedy system and the online law library to get results against those, including staff, who have harmed or violated you, can be complicated and confusing.

I was bewildered just looking at the books and the online law library, and had no idea where to start on my first trip to the law library in pre-COVID times. I was excited, thinking "Great! I'll get some help to settle this detainer." *Nope.*

There are no legal aid clerks to assist you in a federal prison. You must tell them what books or forms you require. Don't know? "Sorry - can't help you" will be the polite response.

This book aims to help you navigate the administrative remedy or grievance process, introduce and explain how to use the online legal library, and discuss exhausting your remedies in preparation for going to court.

I wrote this book so anyone can help themselves. Are you thinking of not having a high school diploma? That's okay. Few to no computer skills? That's okay. No idea where to start? That's okay too. This book simplifies the how-to process, going step-by-step from A to Z — or, in our case, from 8½ to 11. No matter your level of education, computer skills, or legal research skills you bring to the table, you can use this book and begin your own paper trail journey.

The administrative remedy may be called a grievance program if you are in a state prison. I will use both words in this book. I will also use he, she, him, or her.

If you want to go to court about *how* your sentence is carried out - time, conditions, lack of medical, etc. - you must exhaust your remedies first. Several current books on post-conviction remedies, written by Kelly P. Riggs at Freeboard Publishers, are available on Amazon.com to help you. I'll put more details in the Appendix at the end of this book.

Persistence pays off. Knowledge is power. The journey of 1,000 miles begins with a single step.

1

YOU HAVE A PROBLEM

So, you've got a problem? A guard or staff member violated your rights. You can't write your wife, husband, or brother who is in another prison? Peeved at the lack of medical care? Have a trust fund problem? Missing some jail time credits? The federal prison trust fund manages your phone and money accounts.

In every facility, there is supposed to be an administrative remedy or grievance process/program. The administrative remedy program allows you, the inmate, to seek a formal review of virtually any aspect of his or her confinement.

The administrative remedy program is also used to appeal Inmate Disciplinary sanctions, commonly referred to as "shots." You are obligated to attempt an informal resolution of the grievance (problem) prior to filing a formal complaint or request for administrative remedy.

If you file an informal resolution, commonly known as an 8½, with your counselor and they say, The BOP doesn't handle this…write your judge, …say, Okay, I must exhaust my remedies first, and keep filing that BP-9, -10, and your -11. Why bother, you ask. I'm wasting time.

Any motion you file in court after sentencing is called a post-conviction remedy. You may file these motions "pro se" on your own. Most judges and courts will deny your motions, writing you back and stating, "You must exhaust your administrative remedies first."

2

REVIEW OF THE
ADMINISTRATIVE REMEDY PROCESS

This chapter is an overview of the process. Subsequent chapters will go into greater detail on the how-tos of filing your remedy or grievance forms.

Whether you are in a state or federal facility, there is a grievance or, as it is called in the BOP (Federal Bureau of Prisons), an administrative remedy program.

In the federal prison system, there are many program statements. Each program statement determines the exact guidelines and process on how to do various things. All the program statements are online on the law library computer. I will explain how to use the law library (online) in Chapter 4. Every program statement in the BOP is assigned a number. Program statement 1330.18 refers to the Administrative Remedies Program. (See page 92 to read the full program statement.) If you seek a formal, official review on any matter connected to any part of the prison, the Administrative Remedy Program was made for that purpose. You cannot file a BP-9 for someone else. You can help them.

The Administrative Remedies Program applies to you whether you are in federal prison, at a halfway house, or on supervised release (CCC).

The program has three (3) objectives:

It is a way to have your issues looked at by higher-ups in the BOP.

Records are kept in a system called SENTRY online of both accepted and rejected BP-9s, -10s, and -11s. (See Chapter 11 for more details)

Staff will correctly use the Bureau of Prisons' rules and policies.

Every federal facility has people assigned who are responsible for the administrative remedy program. The warden, regional director, and CCM (Community Corrections Manager) are to have procedures for responding to, inquiring into, accepting, and rejecting all BP-9s, -10s, and -11s.

Every BP-9, -10, and -11 is supposed to be entered into SENTRY, whether accepted or rejected. A number called a Remedy ID number is to be assigned. Be persistent in obtaining this number. Why? Here are my and others' stories.

Every BP-9, -10, or -11 is supposed to be checked into SENTRY and assigned a Remedy ID number officially. Does that always happen? Ha-ha, not likely. There are three (3) levels for your BP-10 and two appeal levels. At every level, your request may be responded to or denied.

If no record is made of your BP-9 at the institution where you are housed, your BP-10 will be denied. The regional office will advise you in writing to start with your unit team. Others and I have learned the hard way. This book will save you time and frustration deciphering the BOP's "legalese."

Every institution has an Administrative Remedy Coordinator *and a* clerk. At our FCI, this was a closely guarded secret. The clerk is responsible for all paperwork relating to administrative remedies, both incoming and outgoing, and maintaining the SENTRY index.

Unit managers are to process and ensure that all notices regarding your BP-9, -10, or -11 are given to you (inmate) in a timely manner. The responses may be delivered to you via mail, call, or hand-delivered.

Section 5(b) of the Program Statement-Responsibility states, "Inmates are to use these programs in good faith..." HA! Another joke.

The informal resolution starts the process. (See Chapter 3 for detailed instructions) A three (3) day period - not counting weekends - is allowed per the program statement and policy to respond to or "resolve" the issue. Don't hold your breath on receiving a response in three (3) days. Twenty days is the deadline after the submission date.

A BP-9 is the first of three formal administrative remedy steps in the process. Each form goes to a different place. Each form is a different color and will have a different number of days you must receive your response.

Not receiving a response in a timely manner is considered a denial. Chapter 10 will discuss, in detail, no response.

A BP-9 is blue, used at your institution (or place of confinement), and given to your counselor.

A BP-10 is yellow and is used as the first level of appeal. It is mailed to the Regional Office for your area.

A BP-11 is pink and is the second, or final, appeal inside the BOP. It will be sent to the Central Office in Washington, D.C.

> Note: At the back of this book is a chapter called Appendix. Addresses to determine your region, and more helpful information can be found there.

Only one (1) issue or complaint can be put onto a BP-9. If you list two (2) complaints or problems - even if related - your BP-9 will be rejected. You must include a copy of every cop-out or "8½," any paperwork you have filed trying to resolve this matter, or your BP-9 may be rejected.

Never give the counselor or anyone in the BOP your only copy of papers.

You will take and give one (1) set of paperwork to your counselor at Open House. Every counselor in the BOP is required to provide an open-door policy for you to seek their assistance. In a few days to a week, ask them for the Remedy ID number assigned to your BP-9. Also, ask what date it was entered. Prepare to be persistent.

Have a severe safety or sexual issue? Sensitive matters related to safety or sexual abuse issues don't have to be filed at the institutional level and receive special handling and processing. You will file a BP-10, which will be called a "Sensitive 10," and mailed directly to your regional office or level. The regional office won't return your papers to the prison or where you are housed. Chapter 8 has all the details to help you. No one deserves to be abused - physically, sexually, or emotionally.

Appeals

If you disagree with your warden's response to your BP-9, you can appeal by simply filing a BP-10 to your regional office within twenty (20) days of the date the warden signs the response.

👁 *WATCH HERE* When the counselor calls you into their office to receive your reply, you will be asked to sign a logbook. *Check the date listed as you receive this paperwork!! If it is *not* the correct date, say so, and wait for the counselor to correct the log. This is just another way the BOP tries to be slick. Not all counselors will do this.

You could file an appeal if you filed your BP-10 with the Regional Office and disagreed with their response. You will get a BP-11, copies of all paperwork, and mail them to the Central Office in Washington, D.C.

If you are even thinking about going to court for help, you will need all this paperwork to seek a formal, official review of any matter you give, and some case law on that topic.

You must attach four (4) copies of each attachment, or related paperwork, to your BP-9, -10, or -11. The policy states one (1) copy, but the Regional and Central Offices will require four (4) copies. You must specifically state the reason for the appeal and a recommended resolution on your form.

You can have another person help you fill out the forms, but they cannot do it for you. Family, friends, or an attorney in the free world can also help you.

If you speak another language, are disabled, or cannot read, the prison is supposed to help you. Tell your counselor, in writing, your reason for needing help. As always, keep a copy for yourself.

Rejections or You Must Resubmit

Per BOP Policy §542.17, a coordinator at any level can reject your BP request or appeal. In writing, they must explain why it is being rejected. If it is rejected for a reason because the notice may tell you of the "reasonable time extension in which you must fix and retain your BP request.

Common reasons for rejections include:

- You did not start at the institutional level
- Obscenity - "Don't cuss them out"
- Abusive language
- You did not submit four (4) copies of each attachment
- Not asking for a recommended resolution

Generally, five (5) days on the calendar is the time to resubmit your request at the first step, a BP-9, at the institution where you are housed. Ten (10) calendar days are usually allowed at the regional level. The Central Office may allow up to fifteen (15) days.

Sensitive 10s or 11s

Special handling rules exist for sensitive Bp-9s, -10s, or -11s. If you submit a sensitive 10, it will *not* be returned to you at your institution. This protects you as your matter may involve sexual abuse or be a severe safety issue. You will receive a rejection notice in the mail. It may be vague as to the reason why you filed a BP-9 for your safety. See Chapter 8 for detailed information on sensitive sexual grievances.

Are you appealing a rejection? Per §542.14(d), the policy states you have the right to appeal a denial at any level, whether it is rejected, and whether you can try and correct your BP-9, -10, or -11. Exact details on how to appeal will be explained in Chapters 8 or 9.

You turn in your BP form and start counting the days from the date you gave it to your counselor. That's what the program statement says, right? Not exactly. In the Response Time §542.18 section, your time doesn't begin until your BP-9 is logged into SENTRY.

What did Shakespeare say? "There is many a slip between the cup and the lip," or something like that.

Here's a brief description of your paperwork's initial journey:

Your counselor takes your paperwork to the Administrative Remedies clerk, who decides if your BP-9 is accepted or rejected. Either way, it is to be logged into SENTRY, the Administrative Remedy Index, where your BP-9 will receive a Remedy Index number.

Accepting is the keyword here. What you want to happen won't be accepted if you don't ask for a recommended resolution. There are many other reasons your BP-9 may be rejected.

Once the clerk gets your BP-9, the form should be date-stamped with the date it was received, and the Remedy ID number will be written on your BP form.

That number is just like a license plate on your car. That number is how your BP-9, -10, or -11 is tracked throughout the BOP system. All forms submitted must be logged in, per Section 13, Remedy Process; all submissions shall be entered into SENTRY, whether accepted or rejected, in accordance with the SENTRY Administrative Technical Reference Manual.

Once officially filed, you are to receive a reply from the warden within twenty (20) days, the Regional Office has thirty (30) calendar days to reply, and the Central Office has forty (40) calendar days to respond. Don't hold your breath. Extensions can be given.

Many people have, and still are, filed in the court systems about the BOP not following their policies. You must be persistent, keep a log, and send cop-outs weekly or bi-weekly. On the paper, cop-out, write Administrative Remedies Clerk where it says *TO*.

If you don't know the Clerk or Coordinator's name, it doesn't matter. It will be routed to them. Be sure and keep a copy for yourself, even if you must write it out by hand. Write FILE COPY on yours in the upper right-hand corner.

The Program Statement says, "If the inmate does not receive a response within the time allotted for a reply, including an extension, the inmate may consider the absence of a response to be a denial at that level."

The Program Statement doesn't say that you must have an administrative remedy ID number, and your BP-9 must be logged in to SENTRY to continue forward and appeal at both the regional and central levels. Otherwise, your forms will be rejected, and you will be told to "seek help at the institutional level." The critical point here is that you need your BP-9 entered into SENTRY and a Remedy ID number assigned to proceed.

Now that your BP-9 is date-stamped, logged into SENTRY, and a Remedy ID number assigned, you can count your days.

Two days from your twentieth (20th) day, if you have not received a response, send a cop-out to your warden electronically. I'll show you how to do this here.

1. Go to the main page for Corrlinks, where you keep track of your money, emails, and medicine. Looking at the column of choices on the right-hand side, look for the button labeled "Request to Staff." Click on that.

2. A form appears. In the upper-left box, your first option is to click on the arrow for a drop-down menu of choices. Select Warden. A second way is to type in the word "warden."

3. On the top right side is a box. Here, type in Administrative Clerk/Coordinator.

4. The next option is your job assignment. Type it in.

5. In the big box, you will enter your message. Be brief and to the point.

   Example:

   I turned in a BP-9 form to the Counselor's name in the unit on the date. To date, I am still waiting to receive a response or a Remedy ID number.

   (Skip a line or two here)

   What is the Remedy ID number assigned to my BP-9? What date was it logged into SENTRY?

6. That's all. Click on the submit button. After it is submitted, highlight that request, and click the print button at the very top of your computer screen. A message will appear saying you must pay 3 Trulincs credits. Say yes. Print out your copy.

That is the first step for your BP-9 on its journey.

Next, I will give you an overview of the path that your BP-9, -10, or -11 takes through the system:

1. The Administrative Clerk or Coordinator logs your Request for Remedy into SENTRY, date stamps your actual form, and a Remedy ID number is assigned and should be written onto your form.

2. Every BP-9, -10, or -11 is assigned to staff for investigation and to prepare a response. If your complaint or issue is against staff, those individuals cannot be involved in either the investigation, nor can anyone under their supervision.

3. If your complaint involves abuse - physical, emotional, or sexual, your form will go to SIS (OIA), the Office of Internal Affairs, and is handled differently. Chapter 8 will detail the special handling and coding for a sensitive 10.

4. Any and all information relating to your BP-9 shall be attached or explained in the reports. You won't receive them, but those documents will be in the case file.

5. Your answer, officially a response, will be in the original form. It should tell you what the decision is and give the reasons why. The answer should be complete, "accurate, and factual." If a Program Statement or other rules and regulations are referred to, the numbers for each section mentioned should be included.

Once your response is ready, it is considered "complete," and the SENTRY index will be updated.

You should be given three (3) copies of your response. At the first step, or BP-9 level, files and any information collected during the investigation are kept in the Warden's Administrative Remedy File.

The policy states that if you appeal or file a BP-10 or -11, you must submit one (1) copy of the response with your appeal. You must submit four (4) copies of every paper, or you will receive a rejection notice.

Anyone in the free world can request a copy of your Administrative Remedy per the Freedom of Information Act (FOIA). You will learn how to use the FOIA in Chapter 12.

Many times, in this chapter, I've mentioned the index. The index is the database contained in SENTRY where your grievances or BP-9, -10s, or -11s are listed. Per §542.19, *Index and Response Index*, prisoners and people in the free world can request information and access the Administrative Remedy Indexes and Responses under the FOIA.

The Central Office of the BOP, located in Washington, D.C., must make all indexes of every regional office and each institution available. You must know the Remedy Index number as listed in the index. You must purchase the copy or copies. The amount charged is listed in the FOIA. Currently, fees are $0.10 per page. The first 100 pages are free. The prices are explained in detail in 28 CFR §16.10.

Records have been kept from SENTRY for twenty (20) years and are accessible via computer. The Administrative Remedy case files may be shredded after three (3) full years from the date a grievance is complete.

3

GETTING STARTED
THE INFORMAL RESOLUTION PROCESS,
OR DOING YOUR 8-1/2

You have a problem. You've gone to the staff. You've gone to the mainline. The problem is not resolved. Take notes when you talk to staff. Write down when, where, who, and what the staff says. You've written 3 to 5 cop-outs, officially called Inmate Requests to Staff, for help. You're annoyed, aggravated, and frustrated. What to do? What to do?

First, take a deep breath. Stay calm. Don't feed into staff trying to get under your skin. Second, collect all your copies of cop-outs - whether on paper or electronically. Third, if you have not done so, start a log. Here's how:

1. Take a piece of paper and turn it sideways so that it is wider than longer. The computer calls that landscape.

2. Write "Administrative Remedy Log" at the top.

If you send an electronic cop-out, please remember to print out several copies. You can only print out one at a time. After sixty (60) days, your electronic requests to staff and any responses will disappear into the Black Hole of Internet Space.

At this point in time, you have made a good-faith effort to resolve your problem. You've complied with §542.13 of the program statement. Good job!

Administrative Remedy Log

(A) Issue: _____

_____

_____

(B) Recommended Resolution: (What you want to happen): _____

_____

_____

Date	Whom spoke to/ When, Where	Form Filed	Results/what said

Let's talk about the papers you've accumulated. Buy a manila folder or make a folder out of two (2) pieces of plasticraft and two (2) shoelaces or yarn. If you use shoelaces, you will need to use toenail clippers to make bigger holes in the grid to "sew" your folder together. Here are two (2) versions I have made.

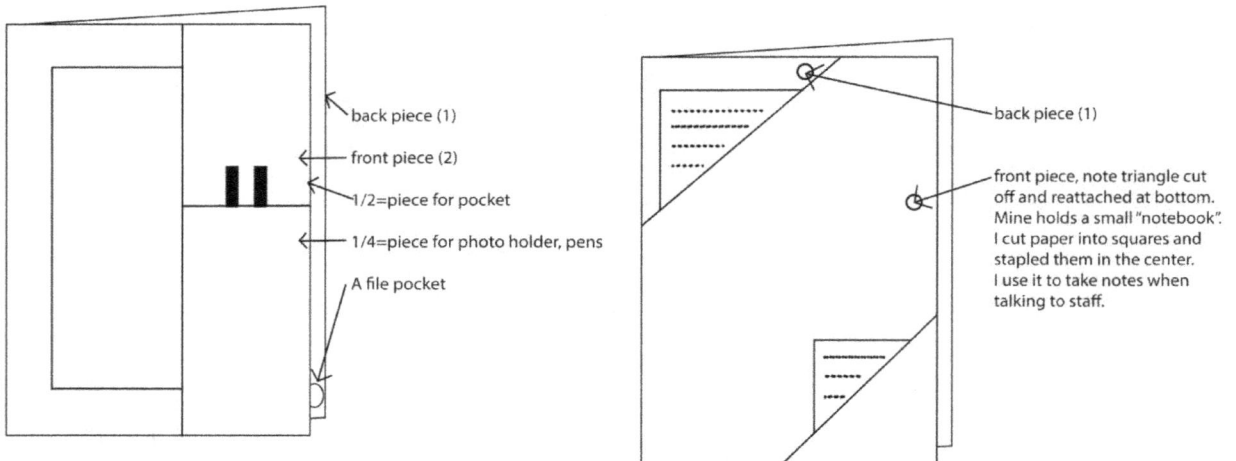

back piece (1)

front piece (2)

1/2=piece for pocket

1/4=piece for photo holder, pens

A file pocket

back piece (1)

front piece, note triangle cut off and reattached at bottom. Mine holds a small "notebook". I cut paper into squares and stapled them in the center. I use it to take notes when talking to staff.

It is time to file your 8½, or Informal Resolution. Go to the open house and see your counselor. Tell them you need two (2) 8½ forms. The counselor will fill in the blank regarding the date. Attach at least one (1) copy of a cop-out.

Officially, "three" days are allowed by the BOP to seek out answers and respond to you. You must go back to your counselor on the fourth (4th) day and perhaps again a week later to find out the results. Be sure to document in your log: the date, time, and any comments made by the counselor. Your response may be verbal and repeat the response back to the counselor to ensure you have the wording exactly. A written response is similar to winning the lottery.

We now have three (3) possible scenarios on what to do next.

A. You see the counselor, and the issue is resolved satisfactorily. STOP. Do the happy dance, but do not throw those papers away. You received a verbal response. Wait until you have something in writing. Staff often will be very reluctant to put anything in writing. Make notes.

B. You see your counselor, and the issue is unresolved: There are two (2) options here.

1. The informal resolution instructions say to go see your Unit Team. If you cannot see them today, file an electronic cop-out *and* a paper one. Why? That oh-so-valuable paper trail.

2. If you see Unit Team and it is resolved - GREAT! If not, go to the mainline. Take copies of the paperwork or a written cop-out with a brief summary of your issue and your requested resolution. Be sure to write in your log if you go to the mainline.

C. The counselor says you must file a BP-9. Get two (2) forms. The blue form is the BP-9. The BP-9, plus attachments - four (4) of each - must be returned to your counselor. Don't date it!!! See Chapter 6 for the next step.

4

USING THE ONLINE LAW LIBRARY

You are interested in looking up cases that may help you get less time? Seeking program statements for RDAP, Disciplinary Sanctions, and the First Step Act? Just want to check out the online law library? This chapter will help you learn to navigate, find information quickly, and identify legal resources that may assist you in reducing or correcting your sentence.

Every facility has a legal or law library. Before COVID-19, you could visit this library. As most of us in prison are on "modified lockdown," that option is not available. An online law library is available on at least one computer in your day room.

Before I go any further, if you need forms, write education, and ask for them by topic or form. It is time to go to the computer room and explore. You are just going to familiarize yourself with finding the online law library. Log in to your account the usual way. Look at the right-hand side of the screen where you check your money and prescriptions. Scroll down the list until you see Law Library. Click on that option. The main screen will appear. It will say "LexisNexis CD Content Selector." You will see a table of contents with a long list of places to explore on your journey. Now look in the upper right-hand corner. See a red "X"? Perfect. Click on the red "X." The next screen will appear. At the top, it will say "Folio Views." Along the top of the screen will be three (3) words:

File	LexisNexis	Help
↳close	↳Content Selector	↳Ha-Ha.
↳Exit	↳Search All Content	

Look towards the middle of this screen page. The words "LexisNexis CD" appear. Below that is a toolbar. A toolbar is a line of tools or options on the computer, often with icons or pictures. I will explain the function of each icon later in this chapter. For now, we're just exploring. Look at the toolbar. See the file folder next to the magnifying glass icon or button. Click on the file folder. A new page will appear. It will say "FBOP-Premium Legal Library Publications List/Contents List." There are quite a few folders to check out later. Look at the upper-right-hand corner next. See the "X"? Click on the "X" to exit this page and return to the previous page.

Locate and click on the magnifying glass button. A form will appear. It will say, "Search All Contents." There is an empty line where you will text or enter your query. A query is defined as "a question, an inquiry." You are querying, inquiring the law library for answers. There are many tips and tricks to help you locate your answers. Don't start typing yet. You can find information quickly by framing your question or keywords with quotation marks. Stop here and check out your keyboard. Find a feel for both the "F" and the "J" keys. Notice a ridge? Now look to the right of the "J" key. The next keys are K, L, :/, and "/" keys. On the left side of the keyboard is a key labeled "shift." You hold that shift key down to make capital letters. You also hold it down whenever a key has two (2) choices. Holding down the shift key will type the top option. You will hold down the shift key and then press the "/" key. A quotation mark will appear. Many people are unfamiliar with a keyboard or a computer. Everyone's skill level is different.

To find information, you will type in a quotation mark, no spaces, then your query or words, then a second set of quotation marks. You can put a space between your words. By using quotation marks, you will narrow and refine your results. You can also type several sets of words surrounded by quotation marks.

This is a shortcut I've shared with many. Using this shortcut at the beginning of your search will help you in several ways. First, it will show you how many files, or areas, in the online law library your query is listed. Second, if your search brings up few or no "hits" or files, you must re-frame and re-think your search words.

In my example, we seek information on a detainer or warrant from another state. Possible search words are: "detainer," "IAD" (Interstate Agreement on Detainers), "pending charge," "arrest warrant," and "Georgia." Notice that each word is framed in quotation marks. The search engine will locate those words in the entire online library. You can also enter a question, sentence, or phrase, again surrounded by quotation marks.

In our example, we have a detainer in Georgia. You have a detainer action letter from R&D. That detainer denies you halfway house time, the benefits of RDAP programming - up to a year off, and raises your blood pressure and custody level. You've clicked the red "X" and are now on the Folio Views page in the law library. Find the magnifying glass icon or button and click on that. You will text or type in a quotation mark, no space, your search words (detainer), then a second set of quotation marks. Click "Find." Wow! We need to narrow down the results. Go back to the text box. Type in quotation marks, no space, detainers, one space, Georgia, no space, and a second set of quotation marks. It will look like this:

Click Find here.

```
"detainers Georgia"
```

Adding a few words can refine your results, saving you endless hours of reading things unrelated to your query or search.

Every law/legal library folder will have icons or buttons with symbols. Let's talk about those next. Not every button will appear in every file. Each icon or button will have a different function. The buttons will appear on a toolbar on each page.

Magnifying Glass icon. A very useful button. You can enter your keywords, a case or Lexis number, a phrase, or a question here. Surrounding your words with quotation marks will narrow your results. The results displayed will list where in the contents you have "hits" or results found.

File Folder icon. Clicking on this button will bring up the table of contents, all the folders available and accessible in the online law library.

Go back button or icon. This button will take you back to the previous screen. For example, you are reading a case, and the law or information is highlighted in blue. You click on it, read the law, and take notes. To return to the previous spot, click on the go-back icon. Please note that this only works if you click on a link that is blue.

Go forward, icon. You clicked on a highlighted line, read the section, and made notes. You clicked the Go Back button. Oops. You reread the section and need to refer to the highlighted section again. Use this button.

Search icon. This button will list all the places you've gone and searched *only* during your current session. By double-clicking on an entry or highlighting the entry and clicking Go To, you can review that item again. Your search won't be saved for use another day.

Advanced Query icon. This button will have an advanced query or search menu appear.

Clear Query icon. It clears or removes your most recent search. You can still find the information in the search history until the end of your session.

Last/Previous Hit icon.

New/Next Hit icon.

You will use these two (2) buttons to steer or navigate through the documents you are reading.

Let's go back to our example. We picked Georgia as our state. You typed in "detainer Georgia." Next, you opened a folder called U.S. District Court 6th District. Look at the toolbar. Notice how these two buttons appear darker and larger than the other set, similar in shape? You will click the New/Next hit icon/button to move forward in this folder. Every time one of your keywords appears on the screen, you will read the surrounding words. Does it apply to your situation? No? Click the Next arrow again and check out the next entry. Don't get discouraged. I've spent many days and found one item that helped. It takes time, and, regretfully, we have that.

If you click the New/Next button twice by mistake, don't panic. Simply click on the Last/Previous button once.

Last Hit Record icon. Next, Hit Record icon.

These two symbols are used to navigate forward and backward to the next record or document, or to the previous record that has your key search words in it.

Zoom icon. You can increase the font or the size of the text using this button.

Bookmark or Tag Record. Clicking on this button adds a red line to the left-hand side of whatever you are researching. It doesn't save this information in a regular database compared to a Google or Yahoo database.

Printer button or icon. Use this button to print. You must highlight the section or sections you want to be printed. To highlight, you put the cursor or arrow before the letter you want highlighted. You drag the mouse, and words will be highlighted. Once you have the section highlighted, go to the print icon and click. It will say you will be charged "x" number of TRULINCS. You must say yes or no. At our FCI, TRULINCS are 5 cents apiece.

Clicking yes moves the pages you want to print to your print queue based on your email account. You must go to the printer, then click and agree to pay in TRULINCS to receive printed documents. The law library and outside rec are where printers are located at this facility.

The Main Screen - Table of Contents

You've got your notebook and pencil ready. You've opened the law library tab on the main page. Slow, isn't it? You see a long list of topics and categories to choose from. The Content Selector is similar to a table of contents. Today, you are exploring. To open one, you simply click in the empty box to the left. A checkmark will appear. You can click more than one folder or option. Lastly, click the open button two (2) times fast - or double click it's called.

To close your choices, click on the exit button or "X" in the upper-right-hand corner of the computer screen. Sometimes you must click 3 to 4 times to exit back to the main page. Did I mention it is a slow o-o-old program?

If you opened a selection and want to search elsewhere without closing that page, go to the toolbar and click on the file folder. The contents list will appear. There is a publications title button that will allow you to go back and forth, or "toggle," between several viewing formats.

Next, exit out of any open "files/folders" you have opened and go back to the main contents page. At the very top is a folder called Contents Description. In this folder is a short summary and description of every source contained in the Contents Library. Imagine a bunch of folders in a file cabinet. The cabinet is the computer.

Before we go any further, I want to reiterate, reset, that not every symbol or button will appear in every document or category that you open. It varies. There will be binoculars or a query button in many federal and state case law folders.

The Supreme Court information folders or database won't have binoculars. I am going to discuss several ways of searching and locating information. You can search using essential keywords, case law, or the actual case itself.

For my example, we will use the case of *Rehaif vs. United States*. It is a case I've looked up several times and can find it in several ways. This case is about a man who was in the United States illegally and was convicted of firearm possession while being in the U.S. unlawfully. The important point is the "knowingly and willingly" possessing firearms part of the law.

The first way we will search is a broad search using the binoculars on the main page toolbar. Click on the binoculars, which is officially called the Query button. A dropbox will appear. You will text or type in quotation marks, no space, Rehaif, no space, and a second set of quotation marks. Tap or hit the enter, find, or search button or key. The computer will rapidly search the database. The listing on the screen will quickly expand for the next few minutes as entries are added. Once the listings stop moving, select one or more files. You can open these by clicking the open selected button in the center and bottom of your computer screen or double-clicking an individual.

This is also called Search All Content - Basic Search. Once your documents are displayed, you will search the document using your new or next backward and forward buttons on the toolbar. You will see two similar sets of symbols. You will use the larger, bolder, or darker set here. This button will jump or move to the next keyword displayed in your document.

You are searching using the advanced search option. A more advanced search option is used if you have more information to enter. Looking at the toolbar, you will see two (2) pairs of binoculars. The pair closest to the left-hand side of the monitor is the symbol or icon for the advanced search option.

There are research tips and tricks you can use to improve the results you receive. Adding the words: and, or, not, or quotation marks (") will change the results. All the tips and tricks I've learned are in Chapter 5.

Citations. You will see this word many times. It is defined as the written reference, which is numbers and letters, to report cases or legal authorities. These are found in legal documents, sometimes called briefs. A citation allows you to locate and view the document or legal authority quoted. Using my example of *Rehaif*, the Supreme Court citation will be *Rehaif v. United States, 139 S.Ct.* 2191 (decided June 21, 2019) Lexis 4199. Another citation for this case is 204 L.Ed. 2d 594 (2019). Rehaif's case is originally from the 11th District of Florida. The appeal case citation is 2019 U.S. App. Lexis 26802 (11th Cir, Florida, Sept 5th, 2019).

Shepardizing

Shepardizing. Often, a case will be reversed, remanded, or overturned by another court. To be sure your case law is "good" law and meets your point of view or requirements, you will go through a process or step commonly referred to as "shepardizing."

Shepards is the name of the database and printed volumes or books. It is a very useful tool to validate and verify your cases. We, in the federal prison system, do not have access to printed or hard copies and can only look online.

You will need the actual number assigned to the paper citation. Every case is shepardized. These numbers are listed in the Federal Reporter or in the federal supplement. You will use the research tips and tricks I'll show you in Chapter 5 to find the actual citations and then go to Shepard's database or file online to locate them.

PREFACE is the information found at the beginning of a shepard file. Many questions about a case may be answered there. The most frequent shepardizing questions I'll discuss here.

Question #1: Why should I shepardize a case?

Answer #1: The decision in a case can be reversed, remanded, or overturned by a higher court. You need to know if this has happened in the case you are quoting as a reference to your case.

Sometimes a statute can be made invalid or unconstitutional. If the case you are referencing has been noted, is criticized, or is limited, you need to know and decide if the facts in your case are similar to or the opposite of those in your case.

Question #2: Which Shepard's database or file do I go into on the computer's online law library?

Answer #2: You must know that the circuit or jurisdiction matches your case. If it is a federal court rule and a federal case, use the federal citations area of Shepards. Where the document or case was shepardized originally is where you will look. Please note that if you are seeking Shepard's case from the District of Columbia (D.C.), there is a D.C. citations section in Shepards.

Question #3: The case numbers in the printed or hard copy version cannot be found in the online reference.

Answer #3: There are two possible reasons why.

> Reason #A: The hard copy list cites the actual page your case was cited, not the first page of the cite. Because of this, use the advanced query option, either the search button on the toolbar or the binoculars that are the farthest to the left of the computer screen. The page numbers will be inside the opinion and not actually in the caption.

> Reason #B: West, as the publisher, may not have sent the hard copy listing to Shepards yet. There may be only a Lexis cite or number listed.

Question #4: What are all these definitions and abbreviations in Shepards?

Answer #4: Read the PREFACE at the front of the Shepard's category or listing. There will be a list of commonly used abbreviations and treatment analysis definitions. The PREFACE will help you to understand shepardizing.

Question #5: Why is one case listed as a reference many times on occasion?

Answer #5: Multiple reporters may report a case. It may be listed regionally and in a state's listing or system. Since it is listed twice, Shepards will list it twice, assigning an individual number to each reporting source.

Are you looking for laws, statutes, or codes?

Laws may be listed in several ways. There is a section online called the Popular Names Table or the U.S. Statutes at Large Table. You will use their Public Law number, or citation, in either table. In either table, you may find the law, but it may not be the most recent version of the law. You must find out when the law was added to the U.S. Code, then review that.

Statutes are commonly referred to as the U.S. Code. A section of public law is just a statute.

There are several ways to search for statutes:

- A general search using a keyword that may be relevant to your issue or topic.

- Using a number, known as the citation, for your specific statute.

- Using the name of your statute.

Here's how to locate your law, code, or statute:

- When opening the online legal library, you will see the Contents Selector page.

- Read or scroll down the titles until you see one called U.S. Code Service (information/database).

- Put a check mark in the empty box to the left by clicking the indicator arrow once.

- At the bottom of the page, it may say open.

- Click there.

- Next, look at the table of contents to the left and check the box where the number you are looking for is located.

- Once that section is opened, go to the toolbar and click the search button.

- A drop-down menu will appear.

- Select the full code search option.

- In the code section, do not put words or symbols — just numbers.

- Skip subsections.

Want to search the Statutes at Large Table next? Also, in this section, there should be a link to the current, updated section of that code in the info base.

Here's the how-to:

> In this example, we will look at the First Step Act, passed in 2018. You do not need to know the year an act passed if searching by name.

- You will open the law library online on the main page, also called Content Selector.

- Scroll down the listings and select both the folders labeled United States Code Service and United States Code Service, including Statutes At Large, Acts by Popular Name, and Table of Abbreviations.

- Click on the OPEN button shown to the right.

- Click on the advanced query button (that is, the binoculars on the toolbar).

- Enter the words (including the quotation marks): "first step act."

- Click Okay.

You should see the listing for the First Step Act of 2018. If you see more than one listing, that Act may have multiple listings. The first one will always be the first codification of the Public Law; then the other ones will be for any time the Act was amended. Please keep in mind that an Act may be partially or totally amended.

For my next example, we will say I don't know the Public Law, so we will go to the Statutes at Large option.

Here's the how-to:

- On the main page of the law library, also called Content Selector, find the U.S. Code Service and the U.S. Codes Tables.

- Put a check mark in the box to the left of both files.

- Click the OPEN button shown on the right.

- Click on the advanced query button, whose symbol is a magnifying glass.

- Enter the words (including the quotation marks): "first step act."

- Click Okay.

- The listing for that Act will be shown.

In our example, it states, "First Step Act of 2018, P.L. 115-391, 132 Stat 5194, 18 USCS §1 nt. The words "P.L. 115-391" are your Public Law number. Now, click on the binoculars on the toolbar and open the advanced query drop-down box.

- Enter the following: "115-391"

- Click Okay.

The computer will show you the listing for Public Law 115-391. It will say the date it was enacted in our example, which was on December 21, 2018. Three columns will be shown next. The first is labeled P.L. Section. Each section or part of the law will be listed. The second column is titled Stat. Page. In our example, it says 132 Stat. 5194. The last or third column is titled USCS Reference. The first list says, "New — 18 USCS 1nt. unclass."

Every public law has two parts or sets of numbers separated by a dash. The first series of numbers relates to the Congressional section in which the law was passed. The First Step Act was passed in the 115th Congressional section.

The second series of numbers tells you the number, or order, the law was passed. Example, 115-391. This law was passed in the 115th Congressional session and was the 391st law passed.

Please only use a hyphen or dash between sets of numbers when you use quotation marks.

If a law is older, it may not have a number. It may have been assigned a chapter law number. The last chapter of the law was Chapter Law 873 on March 3, 1901. At the 57th Congressional session, Public Law 3 was enacted on January 22, 1902.

Forms

There are sample legal forms in two (2) information bases in the online law library. You will look in two (2) places:

- Criminal Defense Techniques
- Bender's Federal Practice Forms

Both folders are organized differently.

The Criminal Defense Techniques has quite a few chapters related to specific crimes. There are generalized motions, including, but not limited to, a suppression motion in the search and seizure chapter.

To find a specific form, enter the word form surrounded by quotation marks. Also, try "sample." Putting another word in front of the word form or sample will help narrow the results. For example, type in:

"Suppression Form"

Bender's Federal Practice Forms go along with the Federal Court Rules. The most commonly used forms will be located under the Federal Rules of Criminal Procedure, Federal Rules of Appellate Procedure, Federal Rules of Evidence, and Post-Conviction Remedies folders.

Under Rule 81 in the Federal Rules of Civil Procedure is information covering a federal habeas corpus. To search, enter keywords.

Seeking A Supreme Court Case

You have a name, citation, or number from a Supreme Court case you are interested in researching. You don't have a date.

Here's how to locate your case:

- Go to the main page of the online law library that says Content Selector.

- Scroll down and put a check mark in the box in front of the listing that says Supreme Court info or database. You can select the one labeled current or present, or select several.

- Click on the OPEN button to the right.

- Find the advanced query button with binoculars on the toolbar and click. A search or drop-down box appears.

- Type in the citation number. In a prior example, we used the *Rehaif* case. That citation is 139 S. Ct. 2191. You will type in as follows:

    "139 S. Ct 2191"

- Then hit enter or okay.

Several results will appear. Ta! Da! See how easy that was! Do you see many cases? That simply means that the case number, or citation, you entered was shared in the print version or online by other cases.

Now let's research and locate a Supreme Court case by name using the example of *Rehaif v. United States.*

- Go to the main page of the law library labeled Content Selector.

- Scroll down and select the folders labeled Supreme Court, current or present. You can select other folders if you wish.

- Click on the OPEN button.

- Find the advanced query icon on the toolbar and click.

- In the drop-down form that appears, type or enter "Rehaif."

- Select enter or okay.

Seeking a case using the Lexis number?

A Lexis number will have the word Lexis followed by numbers. In our example, it looks like this:

2019 U.S. App. Lexis 26802

From the information shown above, 2019 refers to the year the case was decided; U.S. App references the United States Appellate Court; and Lexis 26802 refers to the Lexis case database and the 26,802nd entry. Every district court has an appeal court. Each area has a number. Here's how to locate a case using the Lexis number:

- On the main page labeled Content Selector, scroll until you find the file labeled U.S. Court of Appeals and the year in which the case was decided.

- Put a check mark in the box to the left and click the OPEN button.

- Find the advanced query, or binoculars button, on the toolbar.

- Enter either the entire case citation surrounded by quotation marks or (including quotation marks) type: "Lexis 26802."

- Click okay.

Earlier in this chapter, we discussed forms. Now let's locate those forms. Here's how:

- On the main page labeled Content Selector, scroll down until you see a file labeled Benders Federal Practice Forms.

- Put a check mark in the box to the left by using the cursor and mouse, clicking once.

- For our example, we will be finding a 2255 (federal) or 2254 (state) habeas corpus form.

- Look at the toolbar and click on the word "search."

- In the dropbox that appears, you will see an option called "2 Forms."

- Click on that selection.

- In the empty space or field labeled Search Form Titles, you will enter habeas corpus.

- Click okay.

The number that you see refers to the number of hits, or the number of records, that have been located.

If you are seeking forms from the file called Criminal Defense Techniques, the search steps are nearly the same. Step 1: On the main page, you will select the folder entitled Criminal Defense Techniques. The subsequent steps are the same.

Congratulations!! You have mastered a very important and vital skill.

5

RESEARCH TIPS AND TRICKS

In the last chapter, you mastered how to use the online law library. In Chapter 5, we will discuss tips and tricks that will enable you to search more efficiently.

My favorite tip and trick is the magnifying glass. Using this tip, you will discover all the potential locations of information related to your keywords entered. Here's how to:

- Open the law library to the main page labeled Content Selector.
- Now click on the red "x" or exit button in the upper-right-hand corner. If you exit out of the law library, exit out of your account, and log back in.
- View the toolbar.
- See the magnifying glass icon or button?
- Click on that button.
- In the drop-down box, enter your keywords surrounded by quotation marks.
- Click find.

Wow! The list may lengthen for a few seconds. You can also double-click on an entry. Use the Go Back button to get back to this screen to search for another item listed.

By adding a few special words or symbols, you can greatly increase finding the information you need. These are and, or, not, XOR (either or), quotation marks, a question mark, or the asterisk (*), proximity, and the at (@) symbol.

AND

You want to search for both words and/or a phrase. There are several ways to do this.

First, use a space between the words. Example: detainer Tennessee (you do not have to capitalize words).

Results: any record that has both words will be found.

Second, use the ampersand (&) symbol or the word "and" in your search.

In either case, surround your keyword search with quotation marks at the beginning and the end.

OR

Use or if you are seeking one or the other. Simply type "or" between your keywords, surrounded by quotation marks.

Results: This will bring up all records that have either the words arrest or detainer, or both.

NOT

Let's say you are seeking or want one word but not a related word. You will type in _____, not _____, surrounded by quotation marks.

Results: This search will locate and retrieve the records that contain the first word but not the second word.

An additional tip about "not." Reversing the word order will change the results.

XOR

XOR stands for either or. You are looking for one or the other of your keywords in this search. Using XOR will bring up all the documents and files that contain one keyword or the other, but not both.

" " (Quotation Marks)

Quotation marks are another of my favorite tricks. You specifically want these words in that specific order. You can list several words, each surrounded by quotation marks or a phrase.

If you do not use quotation marks, the computer will think that the space between the words is an "and." Your results will drastically differ or change.

Always use quotation marks when seeking a citation or Lexis number.

Key Word Wildcards

Asterix (*) - A multiple letter or number search uses the Asterix (*) symbol. It will locate and retrieve all the words formed from the first part of a word used before the Asterix. For example, let's enter search*. The results will include searches, searches, and searching. The Asterix may only be used at the end of a word.

Question Mark (?) - The question mark can be used in the middle of a word, as it will change only that specific letter. In the English language, man refers to one male, whereas men refers to many males. For our example, let's enter "m?n" or "wom?n". The search engine will locate all documents containing the words man and men.

Proximity Searches

There are two (2) types of proximity search: Unordered and Ordered. Proximity means nearness. For example, you want to find words that are in a certain range to each other, no matter their order. Example: "debt or interest@10." Using the @ symbol will find all the files that have both words that are within ten (10) words of each other. You must use quotation marks here to get results. This is called an Unordered Proximity Search, as the words may not be in order.

The second way to search is called an Ordered Proximity Search. This will find those words, in that exact order, within the listed or designated number of words to each other. For example, let's enter "debt or interest/10." It will find these words in that order within the number of words specified. You pick the number or range of words. You must use quotation marks to search using this option.

Single versus Multiple File Searches

When you open the advanced query box, you will see two (2) choices or options. One is a box or button labeled ⸢Apply to All⸥ if you click this button, the search will search through all the files in the system. You will need to open each folder individually.

The second option you simply click on the ⸢OK⸥ button. By checking the ⸢OK⸥ button, you will only view what is in that specific file on the screen.

"∅" or "0" (Zero)

Sometimes you may see a zero (∅/0) at the bottom of your computer screen. It is telling you no results were found. That doesn't mean there is no information available pertaining to your search. Changing your keywords, entering the information you are seeking in a different way, and adding or subtracting words will vary the results. Every time I prepare what I want to find in the legal library, I write several keywords and any variations I can think of at the top of a page. Several times during a search, I've discovered new keywords that I write down to research at that moment or later.

Old Searches/History

While you are in a particular file, you can click on the previous button that is located to the right of the binoculars and review other searches - for that session only. The last search made will show up first. It is chronological in order, so the first search of the day will be listed last. This history only works in that database. Once you log out, your searches are deleted and not retrievable.

Looking for Case Law

There is a song that goes, "...looking for love in all the wrong places..." I sang off-key and changed the words to look for case law in all the wrong places. There are many case law data or infobases. You find them by dates, court names, and circuit numbers.

For this example, we will use Tennessee and the district courts and a detainer. Pretend you are looking for cases and the law regarding detainers and Tennessee. On the main legal library page, you will see the words Content Selector. Scroll and read down the list until you see a file labeled U.S. District Court - 6th Circuit. How do you know that those are the court records you are seeking? What is the 6th circuit, you ask, or are you pondering? I made myself a chart with a list of circuit courts and which state belongs to which circuit. Find the state you are researching, and this chart will identify the correct circuit number. Decisions in federal courts, and in many state courts, are listed in several ways: circuit number, court name or branch of court, case number, and by the date decided. You don't need to know all that information to look up a case. You have a name, a state, and an idea of what a case refers to. I'm going to show you how to find that information so that you can help yourself.

1st Circuit	2nd Circuit	3rd Circuit	4th Circuit
Maine	New York	Pennsylvania	Maryland
New Hampshire	Vermont	New Jersey	Virginia
Massachusetts	Connecticut	Delaware	W. Virginia
Rhode Island		Virgin Islands	N. Carolina
Puerto Rico			S. Carolina

5th Circuit	6th Circuit	7th Circuit	8th Circuit
Texas	Michigan	Illinois	Minnesota
Louisiana	Ohio	Indiana	N. Dakota
Mississippi	Tennessee	Wisconsin	S. Dakota
Canal Zone	Kentucky		Nebraska
			Missouri
			Iowa
			Arkansas

If you don't know what circuit your case is from, look at your timesheet, officially called a computation sheet. Your circuit, court district, case number, and judge's name are listed there. Write R&D for a computation sheet if yours is missing, thrown away, or gone.

9th Circuit	10th Circuit	11th Circuit	DC Circuit
Montana	Colorado	Alabama	DC
Washington	Kansas	Florida	
Nevada	New Mexico	Georgia	
Oregon	Utah		
California	Oklahoma		
Idaho & Guam			
Alaska & Hawaii			
Arizona & N. Mariana Island			

Case law is listed from the newest to the oldest date. Many circuits in the online law library will say U.S. District Court (6th Circuit) from 2006 to 2010, for example. Decisions are also listed from the highest to the lowest court levels if the database or folder has more than one (1) level of court decisions or judgments.

You may need to seek a citation or case in multiple places, especially from the Federal Reporter or the Federal Supplement series. These two (2) do not list cases by date or by jurisdiction, which is also known as the where or location of a case.

Case Law Updates or Case Updates

This category includes the latest or newest decisions from all the courts that are listed in the online library. Five (5) data or information bases are included in this category. Updates in the BOP (federal prison system) may be done quarterly, biannually, or yearly. Many appear to be updated twice a year. Keep checking. The categories include the U.S. Supreme Court Reports, the Court of Appeals, District Courts, D.C. (District of Columbia) decisions, and the Military Courts.

Search the same as you do for each topic or keyword search. If you know some information, you can try the case search dropbox. Go to the toolbar, click on the search or the binoculars button or icon. Please note that the binoculars button to the far left is the advanced search option.

Are you seeking cases decided in the Supreme Court? You may need to select or find a citation to locate that case. The search box will give you various types of information you may enter to locate your case.

No citation? There is another way to find your Supreme Court case. Exit out of the Contents

Selector page using the red "x." Notice the magnifying glass on the toolbar? Click on the magnifying glass button. Type in your keywords or case name surrounded by quotation marks. For example:

"Rehaif" "Supreme Court" "detainers" "Supreme Court"

Explore the results. Take note of circuit numbers, any citations shown, and Lexis numbers. If you do not know the names in the case, enter topics related as keywords in the search anywhere option.

Using a Citation Number

If you have the citation or lowercase number, enter that into the find case by citation option in the drop-down box. If you have a citation that has L.Ed. 2d contained in it, enter that as well. Mixing identifying information is permitted here. If you have a Lexis number, enter it also.

Just because a case is added to the case's updated info base does not mean it is added or included elsewhere. The contents selector is available to you while in the BOP; it was designed for lawyers' use. A cite, or citation, from the U.S. or Supreme Court Reporter from a company called West may not be added yet.

On the search toolbar, click and open the search drop-down box. You will see many choices that require you to have information already.

These include:

- Citation
- Party names
- Docket number (also known as a case number)
- Court
- Date
- Attorney
- Judges (include both those who listen to the case and those who wrote their opinion)

There is a keyword search option, also. This search will only search in the folder or category you are currently in.

Add more information to reduce the number of results and increase the possibility of getting what you want. Keep a page for each case you are researching. Add identifying details, mainly including the Lexis numbers, to that case or item.

Legal Abbreviations

Every legal reporting source, or book, has its own abbreviations. Here are the most common I've encountered:

Lexis citations - there are four (4) four parts.

2018	U.S. Dist.	Lexis	9927
1. Year of decision	2a. Court abbreviation	3. Lexis always remains the same	4. Citation number assigned
	U.S. App 2b. U.S. Court of Appeals		

To read this: The case was decided in 2018 by the U.S. District Court and was the 9,927th case entered in the Lexis database.

Federal Reporter

There are two (2) series or sets.

Federal Reporter 1st series F. (ex: 500 F.112)

Federal Reporter 2nd series F. 2d (ex: 500 F.2d.112)

Federal Supplement Recorder

Federal Supplement Recorder 1st Series (ex, 999 F. Supp 2020)

Federal Supplement Recorder 2nd Series (ex, 999 F. Supp. 2d 2020)

Another tip is that knowing which district a case was decided in helps you to locate the folder or database that contains your case and information. If a case was originally in the Tennessee District Courts and you are seeking appeal results, you will check the chart on pages 25 and 26 of this book. Tennessee is in the 6th Circuit, so you will open the folder entitled U.S. Court of Appeals - 6th Circuit.

If you don't know the circuit or district, keep entering keywords or case numbers in any folder you think may be a possibility. Keep track of your efforts. Another method to locate the information is to use the magnifying glass located on the toolbar on the very first page of the online law library.

The U.S. Court of Appeals records are in many files. Where a case is based and when the case was decided determines placement.

Shepards

Does your case or citation come from the Shepards folder or category? If yes, when you type in the citation, for example: "800 F.2d. 111", you will find the case number, the date a decision was made, and the district or circuit. All this information will be at the heading at the beginning of a case. Be sure and use both the period and the quotation marks when you type or enter the information. Otherwise, the computer's search engine may not find the exact match, and you will spend many an hour seeking your information.

Do you have a citation and are unsure of its origin? Where a case comes from is called jurisdiction, which is defined as the legal authority or the range of authority over a case. In this instance, you want to search all the folders. To do so, you will click on the advanced query button or the binoculars to the far left of your toolbar. Enter or type the citation using and including both the period and quotation marks at either end of the citation.

Example: "900 F.2d 999" or "900 f.2d 999"

Don't click the OK button. Click the Apply to All button. What you will see displayed are all the records in the entire law library related to that citation.

Ø Zeros

Some databases or files will show a zero. If you see only results in the 2nd Circuit folders, you will know the case was in one of the states which are included or make up the 2nd Circuit. Those states are Connecticut, New York, and Vermont.

The zeros in other folders just mean no record for that citation is noted in that particular file.

Next, double-click on the results. Be sure and write down the circuit number, state, and district, dates, Lexis numbers, and any other information you feel you may need.

Are you searching for a citation number? Please note that you can only search in that individual database or folder, not across multiple folders, using this method.

In our example, we are still seeking a case in the 2nd Circuit and have the case or citation number. Go to the toolbar after you select the U.S. District Court - 2nd Circuit folder and click the Search button. A drop-down box will appear. One of the fields will say case site. Enter your citation number here. Your quotation marks are needed here. Don't worry about capital letters. Your results will appear.

Did you receive multiple case records? That citation, or case, was shared amongst other cases in the paper versions of that particular reporter series.

Do you have the name or names in a particular case? The names in a case are called a party or parties. For our example, we are looking for a case in the 5th Circuit, and it is called *U.S. v.*

Witherstone. On the main law library page, at the content selectors page, click to enter a checkmark in the box to the left of the folder called 5th and 11th Circuit, or just the 5th Circuit folder, and click on the OPEN button.

Go to the toolbar and click the search option. In the drop-down box, you will enter or type in:

"witherstone money"@10

That will tell the computer's search engine you are seeking a case with the keywords Witherstone and money. Also, if the keywords are within 10 (ten) words of each other, click okay.

You will get the case specified, plus any references to the case in your results. Use the blue-highlighted citation links to view the results.

A second way is to enter the names involved in the case surrounded by quotation marks. Click on the OK button, and your results will appear. If the last name is commonly used, enter a first name as well.

If a state agency is listed as one of the parties, enter that also. Using a state agency by itself will drastically multiply your results with cases of no interest to you.

Frequently Referred to BOP Program Statements and Numbers

Below is a list of BOP Program Statements and their number for your convenience. There are many more program statements available in the online law library.

P1320.06 Federal Tort Claim

P4500.08 Trust Fund/Deposit Manual

P5212.07 Control Unit Programs

P5214.04 HIV-Positive Inmates Who Pose a Danger to Others

P5264.08 Inmate Telephone Regulations

P5270.09 Inmate Discipline Program

P or PS 5324.12 Sexually Abusive Behavior

and 5324.11 Prevention & Intervention Program

PS5050.50 Compassionate Release/Reduction in Sentence (briefly mentions the First Step Act)

P5890.13 SENTRY - National Online Automated Information System

Certified Mail with Return Receipt Requested

If you ever file in a court or send a letter, and want proof, official documented proof that it was sent and received, then certified mail, return receipt requested is the way to go. It is accepted as proof in any court in the United States. We'll go through this step-by-step.

Mailing a business #10 size envelope with a certified return receipt option currently, as of 2023, costs $7.90 or twelve (12) forever stamps above and beyond the cost of mailing the envelope. You must write the mailroom and ask for three (3) certified mail receipts and three (3) green cards. If the mail room makes regular visits to your housing unit, get in line. Also, ask for a bubble wrap or a priority mail cardboard envelope as well.

There are two (2) parts to each set of certified mail: one is a green postcard, and the other is a certified mail receipt, which is on white paper. The Post Office numbered these forms, and they are officially PS Form 3800 and PS Form 3811.

First, look at the certified mail receipt. It is the flimsy white paper one.

1. Look at the lower right side of the form. Where it says postage and postage due, put nothing - leave it blank.

2. Now, looking at the bottom of the form, see where it says, "sent to"? Write very small, and *PRINT*, fill out where the letter is going. Use names, Clerk of Court, Whatever County Courthouse, Prosecutor, or District Attorney's Office; then neatly write the address, city, state, and zip code.

3. Wiggle the paper, looking to the left-hand border. You will see a dotted line. Above that is a long, long number on a tear-off sticker. Below the words, Certified Mail is a bar code. Below that is a perforated line. Fold and separate the two pieces. *SAVE IT*

4. Set aside the two pieces of PS Form 3800, or the flimsy white form, for now.

5. Let's examine your green postcard, officially called PS Form 3811. The front has a bar code that the United States Postal Service uses to track the package or envelope. The top upper right corner has a stamp that says first-class postage and fees paid. There is a large blank box in the center. You are the sender. Here, carefully, neatly, and in printing, write your name, number, and address.

6. Flip over the green postcard. On the left, it will say "Article Addressed to." In tiny print, neatly write who the envelope is going to, just as you did on the certified mail receipt.

7. At the spot labeled Article #2, you will remove the top sticker from the certified mail receipt. That is the one above the bar code, above the words certified mail. Remove this identifier sticker and place it onto your green postcard at the spot labeled Article #2.

8. Now, let's look at the service type. You check the boxes you want. I checked the certified mail and return receipt options.

9. Both of your certified mail parts are ready. Before you place them onto an envelope, you must label your envelope differently to accommodate seven stamps, plus the white paper portion of the certified mail receipt, plus your return address, and the address it is going to. Get the mailing address out now before we go on

10. a) Pre-COVID, once upon a time, the BOP required you to use a return address sticker. If you have a sticker you want to use, place it as close to the upper left-hand edge as possible.
b) Address your envelope. Put the paperwork in and seal the envelope.

11. Fold your certified mail receipt - the flimsy white part - on the dotted line, where

indicated.

12. You will place this part as close as you can, even over the empty part of your address label. Once you are sure of where it is going to be placed, remove the sticker on the back and add it to your envelope.

Below is a drawing of the front of an envelope, for example:

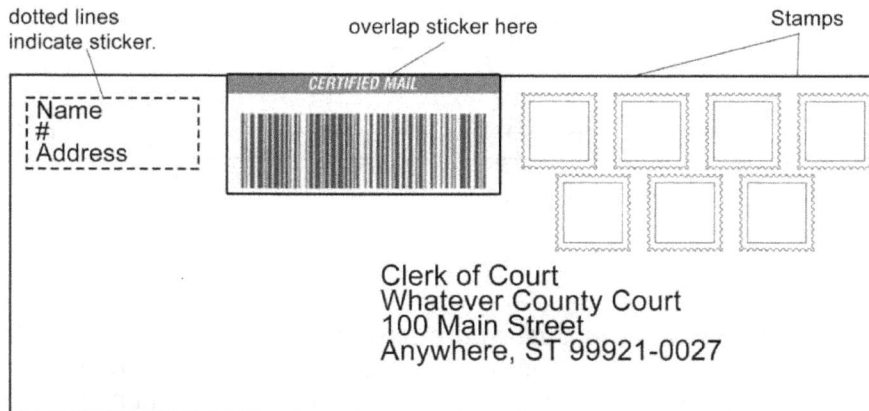

13. Add your twelve (12) Forever stamps starting in the uppermost right-hand corner. You will end up with two rows, and that is okay. Just be sure you can read both the certified mail sticker and the address to which the letter is going.

14. a) Turn your envelope over. Pick up your green postcard. Look at the side that has your name and address on it. At the outside edges are two (2) white strips of paper. Underneath is adhesive. Don't tear off the white strips yet. Just a little more, and you are done.

b) Once you tear off the white paper, you will affix or place the green postcard onto the back of your envelope, in the center.

c) The back of your envelope will resemble my drawing:

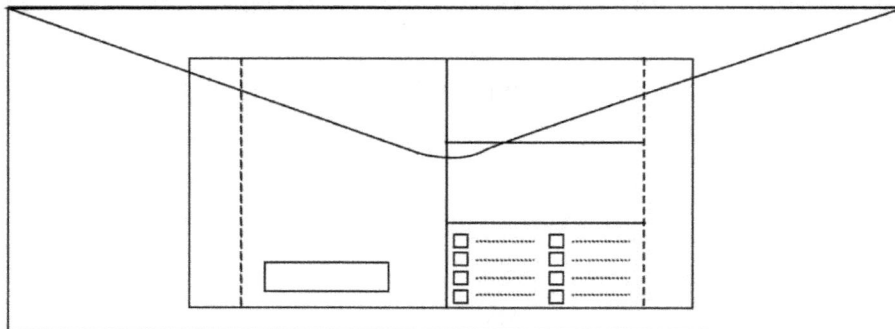

The last step. Write in your mail log the date you mailed the papers, to whom - Court Clerk, Prosecutor, Lawyer, etc. - and the identifier number on the sticker. If your institution does not have a prison mailbox, be sure and note the officer's name and the time you hand it to them.

Your letter will be processed at the Post Office, the same as any other letter, until its last stop: the Postman's delivery bag.

When your letter is delivered to the United States Post Office, the worker will hand it the envelope with the back showing. Whoever receives it must sign for it. The postman will date it with the date received. Next, the postal worker will remove the green postcard from the envelope and give that person the envelope. The green card, the postal person will retain. Once they arrive back at the post office, the green card will be mailed back to you. Save that green card!! If anyone ever says you never notified or wrote them, or they did not receive your paperwork, that card is official proof acceptable in courts.

In the free world, you can use the long, long number on the certified mail receipt to track your envelope. It is unique to that particular piece of mail. Using only that number, the Post Office can track and locate the delivery of your letter online at www.upsp.com or by telephone.

The green card is officially called a Return Receipt.

Printing Your Documents Using Trulincs

You can type, compose, and print documents from your Trulincs or email account. You can also print out emails, requests to staff, notices on the bulletin board, and account or money statements. Check out your email account. On the top left-hand side, it says "To:" Towards the middle, you will see the word "Draft." Click on the draft option. A new main page will appear. You must enter a recipient in the "To" line. The next line is the Re: or email heading line. Are you writing the President for clemency? Type in the President's letter - clemency. Typing a Motion to Dismiss? Enter that.

Write your first draft and click the SAVE button. Later, you can review your letter and revise it as needed, or add to your letter or motion when you have time.

Before you can go to the printer and hold a paper copy in your hands, you must put your email documents or account statements into your print basket.

Emails and requests to staff are only accessible for 60 days before they disappear into the Black Hole of Space. Here is how to mark your documents to print. You may only print one copy at a time. You can print a document multiple times. If you send an email, you can print it, too.

While your email account is open, look at the toolbar. See the printer symbol or icon? Click it. A message will pop up saying it will cost X number of Trulincs to print. Usually, it is 3 Trulincs per draft or email page. You must accept. Your document is sent to the print basket now.

Every institution has a printer for inmates. At our FCI, one is in the law library, and one is at the mainline. Yes, it costs Trulincs. Check out the print basket in the unit. The number of pages will be shown in the column to the far right. Multiply that times 3 to arrive at the number of Trulincs you need to print. If you go to print and are short of Trulincs, you can go and add more then and there and finish printing.

If your institution is on lockdown due to COVID-19 and you cannot access the printer, fill out a BP-199. Write legal copies on it. Give it to your counselor or unit manager. Send a cop-out to Trust Fund advising Trust Fund you need legal copies; it is court-related and time-sensitive.

6

ADMINISTRATIVE REMEDY TIMELINE & STEPS

Does your problem concern a disputed phone charge, and you are asking for reimbursement? Have you written Trust Fund? Filed an 8½, an informal resolution request? Be sure and include the date and time of the disputed call. You can print out your phone records.

First, some background. A lawsuit called *Washington v. Reno* was filed and won. There are specific rules and different time frames for phone bill problems. You have 120 days from the date of the call or the amount in question to file a BP-9. Need more time? If you are in transit, sick, and cannot access your documents, or if it takes a long time to receive a reply to your 8½, you can receive an extension per §542.19. Try to get the staff to put something in writing about the delay. If they laugh at you, file an electronic cop-out stating you need the reason for the delay documented in writing per §542.19.

To access and print your telephone records, follow these steps.

On the main email and computer page to the left is where you access your email and print from. To the right, the top button says Manage Trulincs. The second button says account transactions. Click to open that file. Look under the dates on the file folder tabs. Reading from left to right, the tabs are labeled "Commissary Transactions," "Telephone Account Statements," "Trulincs Transactions," and "Media."

As yours is a phone bill issue, click on the second tab labeled telephone account statements. Now look directly above the date range. You are going to change the date to a few days before and after the date in dispute. Click on the button labeled Search all locations if you were in transit or moved. Click the button labeled $\boxed{\text{Refresh}}$. Any calls made during those dates will be listed along with the number dialed and the amount of the call. Next, look in the lower right-hand corner. Click the button that says $\boxed{\text{Mark for Print}}$. A screen will appear, and you must agree to pay Trulincs.

Once you print the first copy, either use a copy card to get more copies or repeat this process until you have four (4) copies of each bill.

You will file your BP-9 the same way as any BP-9, keeping in mind that you must file within one hundred twenty (120) days from the date of the disputed call.

Timeline & Steps

	Step	Form	Time Frame for Response	Who gets your form - by hand or by mail	Remedy ID #/SENTRY entry
1	Request to Staff (cop-out) - electronic or paper	Yes	N/A	Either by hand or via institutional mail	No
2	Informal Resolution (8½)	Yes	3 days	Counselor - by hand	No
3	BP-9	Yes (Blue Form)	20 days	Counselor - by hand	Yes - ask for a number a week later
4	BP-10 Regular	Yes (Yellow Form)	30 days	Regional Office*	Yes
	Sensitive - special handling	Yes (Blue Form)		Pass steps 1-3 and mail directions to Regional Office	Yes
5	BP-11	Yes (Pink Form)	40 days	Central Office*	Yes

* See the appendix at the back of this book for addresses.

7

Here we are, several weeks later, and your problem has not been resolved. I know it is aggravating. As you realize from the timeline in Chapter 6, every step has a time limit. You've written cop-outs, kept a log of events, and filed an informal 8½. Your counselor has advised you that they cannot fix the problem. Right then, ask for two (2) BP-9s and two (2) BP-10 forms. If possible, pick up the forms in advance.

Drafting and Writing Your BP-9:

You must draft and write your issue, concern, or problem, plus the recommended resolution, on one form. You are allowed to attach an additional page if needed. You can only put or address one (1) issue per BP-9. If the problem overlaps several areas and all are closely related, it may or may not be rejected. It will most definitely be rejected if you put more than one (1) matter on your BP-9. You will be told to fill out a separate form for each issue.

Recommended Resolution:

You must write what you want to be done and how you want this issue resolved on your BP-9 form, and at every level, or it will be rejected.

Continuation or Additional Page to Your BP-9:

If you need more space, you are allowed to attach a piece of paper that is 8½ x 11". You must write "Continuation Page" at the top of the page along with your name and number. You will need four (4) copies.

Exhibits:

You will need four (4) copies of any attachments. The cop-outs, informal resolutions (8½s), and any other documentation should all be labeled at the top as Exhibit A, Exhibit B, and so on. Keep copies of all that you hand over or mail in. Per Section §542.15 (b)(3) of the program statement, exhibits and/or copies most likely will not be returned. If your BP-9 is accepted, the copies will be used to investigate your grievance or remedy request. If rejected, your copies will be returned.

Dating and Signing Your BP-9:

Section 4 of the program statement for administrative remedies says, "shall sign and date the Request and submit it to the institution staff designated." DO NOT date it until you are in front of your counselor. Ask if you can date and sign. If they say yes, sign and date, making an entry in your administrative remedy log. If they say no, verify if they do not want both the date and signature. Make a note in your log that Mr. or Ms. X said not to date or sign. List time, date, and witnesses.

Are you as confused as I was when this first happened to me and others? We all know the BOP has two sets of rules: 1) the official rules and 2) what the BOP really does. The policy clearly says to date and sign. At my FCI, as at others, the staff doesn't want you to date it for several reasons. First, the BOP can lie (GASP!) About when it was received. Second, your BP-9 may lie on a desk for several weeks untouched. You write a cop-out to the Administrative Remedies Clerk - hey, where's my BP-9? What is the SENTRY ID number? Many times, your status cop-out will trigger the BOP to enter your BP-9 into SENTRY, starting the process. At this point, the BOP will enter a date a day or two in advance of entering your BP-9 into SENTRY. No, you gasp; the BOP falsifies paperwork. Yes, it happens frequently. More frequently, BP-9s are thrown away by staff.

Is your issue or problem sensitive? Relate to your safety? Is someone physically or sexually abusing you? First, it is not your fault. Second, you do not have to file at the institutional level where you are physically at. It is called a sensitive 10.

Go to your counselor and say you want two (2) BP-10s. You do not have to give a reason why. In some facilities, these forms are on a rack on the wall. The ones you are looking for are yellow.

Stop here. Go to Chapter 8 and read everything you need to know about sensitive 10s.

Did the counselor just call you to come and sign a log to receive your BP-9 response? *STOP AND CHECK THE DATE IN THE LOG!!" Frequently, the BOP "fudges" the dates on when inmates receive responses to BP-9s or legal papers. It will not be the current date. If you read the date and it is incorrect, politely say the date is from last week, and ask them to correct it. Stand firm and be persistent. The counselor will huff and puff but eventually fix it. If they say sign or don't get your BP-9, ask for two informal 8½ and two BP-9s. The date you receive the response is important if you need to appeal the BP-9 reply.

Appeal

You've battled with the counselor, who unhappily fixed the date in his or her log. You head back to your bunk, stopping to read the response. WHAT!! Of course, we all know that the federal government and the BOP never distort the truth. The program statement calls the next step in the administrative remedy process an appeal, commonly referred to as a BP-10. You are filing an appeal when you disagree with the response given on the BP-9. The paperwork will be mailed to the regional office. Every institution has a regional office. I've listed all the institutions, FCIs, FDCs, and Camps by Regions in the back of this book in the Appendix. Try not to fall off your bunk, laughing at my drawings of states and regions.

Are you housed in a controlled unit and disagree with the BP-9 decision? You will also file at the

Regional (BP-10) Office; then, your BP-11 will be sent to the Central Office. There are program statements called Control Unit Programs and Inmate Discipline Programs that you want to review before filing.

8

APPEALING YOUR BP-9, OR FILING YOUR BP-10

Let's discuss the BP-10 first. There are two types of BP-10s. The first one is the regular BP-10 you file after receiving an unsatisfactory response to your BP-9. It is officially an appeal. I get very irate over the replies I and others have received. Or when you don't receive a reply, move on to the next step and get told to file at the institutional level. Uh-duh! Did that. Where do you think all these copies came from? Egypt? Let me get back on track here...

The second type of BP-10 is a "sensitive 10." Your problem is sensitive. Your safety will be in danger if you file a BP-9. You are very worried that if word gets out that you filed a BP-9, you'll be in danger or dead. You will use the regular BP-10 form, write the word "SENSITIVE" at the stop, and clearly state in the BP-10 why you believe it is a sensitive issue, concern, or problem. You will mail it to the Regional Office directly without passing go or filing a BP-9 where you are housed.

I will make an exception here to make a copy of everything for yourself here. If you are getting abused in any way, shape, or form, your locker may not be a place to keep copies. Is there anyone outside you can mail a set of copies to? I understand you may be too embarrassed or ashamed to let anyone know what is going on. *It is not your fault*!

The Regional Office will either accept or refuse your sensitive BP-10. If they don't accept it, you will only receive a rejection letter by mail, call, or from the counselor or unit secretary. The paperwork you filed will be retained at the Regional Office, so do not worry about the papers being returned or someone reading them. The BOP does get that right, at least. The rejection reason may be vague to protect you.

Don't feel you are done if it is rejected. First, does it say why? Does it say to fix or change something and return it? No. Then you can refile by putting all in an envelope and mailing it directly to the warden via the mail.

Another option is to email SIS or the PREA/OIG (Office of Inspector General) about your problem. There is no record of your email to either SIS, PREA, or the OIG kept in your email file. How do I know this for a fact? I emailed myself to be sure. As soon as you click the ⌷Submit⌷ button, it quickly disappears.

Forms, Forms Everywhere, a Form

Go to your counselor and ask for two (2) BP-10s. Officially, the form is called a Regional Administrative Remedy Appeal. BOP is yellow in color and has three carbon pages plus the original page, for a total of four (4) pages.

Chapter 6 has a chart that discusses times to submit, to whom to submit, and where to submit.

Per the program statement, Section §542.15, if you don't like or agree with the response to your BP-9, you have twenty (20) calendar days to appeal. When do those twenty (20) days start? The policy says twenty (20) days from when the warden signed it. Some regions will start twenty (20) days from the date you receive it. This is where your administrative remedy log will come in handy.

If you have a valid reason for not being able to file in a timely manner: you have COVID-19, were moved and unable to access your documents, etc., you can ask for an extension. Try to get something in writing. If nothing else, and the staff is useless to your requests for help/documentation, fill out either an electronic cop-out/or a paper cop-out to the warden. State in it:

> I need an extension of time to file my BP-10 due to *listing your reasons why you are here,* per the Program Statement, Section §542.15(b). I'm going to quote the exact wording here:
>
> > "When an inmate demonstrates a valid reason for delay, these time limits may be extended."

That is all you need to write. Be sure and keep a copy for your records. Update your administrative remedies log. If you filed an electronic cop-out, print out two (2) copies.

Please don't wait until day eighteen (18) to mail your BP-10 unless it's necessary. It must be received by that date, the twentieth (20th) day. If you must send it late, include a cop-out to the warden asking for an extension.

In my example, we are saying we did not get all our jail credit, and, eventually, you are going back to court. First, you must "exhaust your administrative remedies." That is following the administrative remedy process by filing a BP-9, -10, and -11. You are on step 2 of 3. I call it the paper trail. Chapter 13 will go into greater detail on exhausting your administrative remedies and provide you with some case law you may find useful.

You have your two (2) BP-10 forms. You have made or are going to the law library or counselor, unit secretary, or unit team for copies. Be sure and pick up a few more BP-199 forms to fill out, so the Trust Fund can charge you for copies.

The Program Statement Section §542.15 says one copy. Buzzer sounds here. The Regional Office will reject it without four (4) copies of every page.

Writing Out Your BP-10

This can be tricky. First, you must say you are appealing to the BP-9 decision. Your wording on the BP-10 must closely, or exactly, repeat the wording on your BP-9. Only one (1) problem with an administrative remedy. Write small and inside the space provided. If you need to, you can attach one sheet of paper that is 8.5x11" on which you write at the top, in big letters, boldly, **"CONTINUATION PAGE BP-10."**

You need to press hard as you write. There are three carbon pages below. Be sure to write *Recommended Resolution,* underline, and state what you want to happen. Using our example of missing jail credit, you may say: Please credit me with an additional 10.5 months, or 280 days, of jail credit time.

Put all your copies into four (4) sets, one on each page. Some people put them in order from oldest to newest. Some put the BP-9 copy first, attachments, 8½, and then their cop-outs. There is no hard and fast rule, so you decide. The BP-10 will go on top. Be sure to date and sign it just before you mail it out.

You will need a manila envelope to mail all those papers or a Priority envelope from the mail room—the Priority envelope costs $9.65 or 15 Forever stamps. The manila envelope may take up to $5 to $6, depending on the weight.

Sending it by certified mail and return receipt requested will cost an additional seven stamps. Chapter 5 has a step-by-step guide on certified mail. The green card is proof that your paperwork was received. You will receive the green postcard back by mail call several weeks later. I did not send my BP-10 or 11 via certified mail. That is a personal preference and decision. If you are unable to go to the mail room for supplies like us, send a cop-out and ask for 2 or 3 of each item.

Sexual abuse. PREA. I want you to remember it is not your fault. Per Policy and 28 C.F.R. §115.6, the BOP cannot set a time limit on when you file a grievance about sexual abuse. The BOP has special rules for grievances dealing with sexual abuse.

At any time, you can file a grievance about sexual abuse. Stick to the one issue per grievance rule. If not, the only part of your grievance, as it relates to sexual abuse, will be accepted. Any other issues in your grievance will be rejected, and the "regular" rules apply. You don't have to go into great detail about the abuse unless you are comfortable doing so. Saying an officer pinned me in a shower and raped me is enough. Or four inmates beat and raped me in the shower, corner of the recreation yard, is enough. If you were afraid to seek medical help for fear of retaliation, say so.

You do not have to file an 8½, the informal resolution, or a BP-9 for sexual abuse. Your grievance will not be given to the staff who abused you. Nor will it be given to staff who are supervised by the abuser or involved with that person.

There are two (2) internal prison police or authorities inside the BOP. One is the OIG, Office of the Inspector General, which handles physical or sexual abuse allegations. The other is SIS, who are on the grounds and handle drug problems as well as investigate many things.

The policy allows ninety (90) days total to decide on sexual abuse claims. That ninety (90) days starts the day of filing the claim. Add five days for mailing time. OIG or SIS can ask for an extension of time up to seventy (70) days. You can write back, saying no, the abuse is ongoing.

Keep reading if you need an emergency and expedited grievance.

For sensitive or sexual abuse grievances, as with any grievance, if you do not get a reply back in the time frame specified and allowed per policy, no response is considered to be a denial. Chapter 10 gives information on that subject.

You have the option to receive outside help (family, friends, and legal help) to assist you in filing your BP-10 that relates to sexual abuse claims and "allegations." Per policy, outside family, friends, and legal help can file the paperwork on your behalf *only* for sexual abuse grievances. They can call the Regional Office for your area or the Office of the Inspector General as well to help you.

You must put in writing that you, the injured person, want and agree to have this filed on your behalf and that you may have to take other steps on your own. Date and sign the paper.

If you, the victim, do not agree in writing with anyone else filing for you, the BOP and any other agency involved will document that decision as well.

Emergency and Expedited Grievances

You are getting sexually assaulted. You can't get away. You need to file an emergency expedited grievance.

Section §115.52(f) provides for an emergency and expedited grievance in this case. Your complaint will be processed quickly. 28 C.F.R. §542.18 states, and I quote, "an expedited BP-9 response shall be provided if a remedy (response) is determined to be of an emergency nature which threatens the inmate's immediate health or welfare."

I want you to stop here. Email PREA/OIG right now and explain the situation. I know it's upsetting.

Get a BP-9 form. You don't have to explain why. Write **EMERGENCY** at the top in big, bold letters, underlined. You must state why it's an emergency. You must make a recommended resolution: you want the sexual abuse to stop *now*. You will place this form in an envelope and address it to the warden. You have two options here.

A. You have filed an emergency grievance. Whoever does administrative remedies, either the clerk or the coordinator, will decide if your problem really states a big risk of immediate sexual assault. If the administrative clerk or coordinator agrees that it does meet the rules for a remedy/response that it is an emergency, the request is accepted and processed as an emergency.

B. Your issue is sensitive and sexual, and you're afraid for your safety. You fear you're in danger if this grievance is publicly known at the institution. You can file it directly to the Regional Office. You will still use a BP-9 form. Write **EMERGENCY** in big, bold letters at the top, underlined. Be sure to state *why* it's an emergency — the sexual abuse is ongoing. For your recommended resolution, write, "I want the sexual abuse to stop today, now." Date and sign it. Pop it in the institutional mailbox to your regional office. In the section labeled Appendix, you will locate your institution and the Regional Office's address.

C.F.R. §542.14(d)(1) discusses this issue in great detail.

> NOTE: If you file a false sexual abuse or sensitive grievance to get back at staff, or in bad faith, or to manipulate someone, you can get a shot or disciplinary write-up.

While your sensitive or sexual BP-9 or BP-10 is being processed, it will not be logged in until someone answers it. When your grievance is entered into SENTRY, the online database for tracking grievances, it will be coded vaguely to help alleviate your worries.

If your grievance fails to meet the standards for an emergency and expedited grievance, it will be rejected. You will receive a rejection notice, and the BP-9 or BP-10 will be processed in the usual manner.

Within 48 hours, you are to receive a reply to your emergency and expedited BP-9. Within five (5) days, you should receive a response to your BP-10 and BP-11. If you did not receive a response, take that as a denial and move on to the next step. Always "CYA" and cover yourself when the BOP fails to respond. Send a cop-out, in this case, to or on the PREA/OIG electronic request to staff. No record of it will be kept in your emails. You don't have to put details. If the abuse is ongoing, say so!! Be sure and say ongoing sexual abuse by staff/inmate/bunkie. Go to the mainline and directly ask the warden about your emergency BP-9 sex abuse if you are comfortable talking to the warden in public. Be sure and have a reason ready if someone asks you why you spoke to the warden. Lie. For example, I filed a grievance about missing good time credit and no medical care. If pressed for details, say you don't want to talk about it and walk away. Pay attention to who is around, listening.

Does your sexual abuse involve staff? When your BP-9 or BP-10 is investigated, staff and those who report to or are involved with that staff member are allowed into the investigation. SIS and the OIG may talk to you. If anyone questions you about why SIS is talking to you, say the mail room stole your money order and didn't send it to the lockbox, that it was cashed here in the city you are in.

Help in Filing BPs

You are sick, can barely read/speak another language, and need help? Per Section §542.16, you can get help from another inmate or staff member to assist you in filling out these forms. Shaking your head and thinking I am delusional — staff won't help. You're right; asking staff for help is useless, no matter what the program statement says. You want that paper trail that you did, indeed, ask for help and were ignored.

The program statement also says someone, anyone, outside the prison can fill out the forms. The catch is that no one else but you can file it or turn it in. You cannot go over your twenty (20) day limit without asking for an extension.

If someone else fills out the forms, be sure to write on your BP-9, -10, or 011 that you are sick, have learning difficulties, or English is a second language, and are seeking an extension of time in filing your paperwork. You still need four (4) copies of all your paperwork. If this is mailed to you, be sure to sign and date it before you mail it to the Regional or Central office.

Hablo Espanol? Not functional or fluent in English? The warden is supposed to give you help. Fill out a cop-out, either online or in writing, to the counselor and explain that you need help to do your BP-9, -10, or -11 in Spanish. Here is the Spanish version, courtesy of Sophia, a Spanish-speaking lady:

> "Necesito ayuda para llenar mi 8½, BP-9 o BP-10, no estoy capacitada para escribir en inglés, pero la póliza dice que puedo obtener ayuda.
>
> Gracias"

9

At a mail call, you receive a reply to your BP-10. Or the counselor or unit secretary called you for legal mail. *STOP* Check the date written down to be sure it is *today's* date, not backdated. You may be one of the lucky few whose counselor or unit secretary actually does their job. In this case, I'm happy for you. Still, check that date. Now sign your name and receive that paperwork. Try to bite your tongue so you don't say anything the staff can write you up for. Breathe and count to 10. Ask for two (2) BP-11 forms before you walk out of the counselor's office to rant and rave as you read the response to your BP-10.

Are you satisfied with the BOP's response? GREAT!! Save that paperwork, just in case.

Are you dissatisfied, to put it nicely, with the response you received? On to the third and final step of this process. Your next step is to file an appeal of the Region's decision to the Central Office. Form BP-11, pink in color, will be used. It is officially called the Central Office Administrative Remedy Appeal form.

You have 30 calendar days from the date the Regional Director signed your BP-10 to submit your appeal, commonly called a BP-11. This time frame can be extended for various reasons: you have COVID-19, you cannot get legal copies due to the COVID-19 lockdown, or you are sick or have moved and are unable to access your documents. Try to get a note from the staff stating these reasons. I know, I know, it's like pulling teeth. Go to the mainline. Take two (2) written requests to the staff/warden. On one, in the upper right-hand corner, write "File Copy." On the form, write:

> "I need a time extension in filing my BP-11 to Central Office for the following reasons: *list your reasons here. Please keep it simple*. I require a written response per Section §542.14(b) and Section §542.15."

Section §542.15 of the Administrative Remedy Program Statement says, and I quote:

> "When the inmate demonstrates a valid reason for a delay, these time limits may be extended."

Section §542.14(b) gives valid reasons for delays.

Reply or Response Time

It is stated in Section §542.18 that a BP-11 is "considered filed on the date it is logged into the Administrative Remedy Index as accepted." A BP-11 must be responded to by the Central Office or General Counsel within forty (40) calendar days.

Did you file an emergency BP-11? Are you threatened? Is your immediate safety and well-being at risk?

If yes, your response should be received within three (3) calendar days after filing.

The policy states that you must submit at least one (1) complete set of copies. Submit four (4) complete sets, or your BP-11 will be rejected, and you will have to send it again. I realize it is getting expensive - all these copies, manila envelopes, and postage. Many counselors will hate to see you coming. The COVID-19 crisis has made a lot of extra work for them and us. Be firm, be persistent. State your issue repeatedly: I need legal copies, and it is a time-sensitive matter.

The Central Office can grant you a twenty (20) day time extension. The Central Office can also request an extension of time from you of up to twenty (20) days. You have the option to write the Central Office and advise them that you don't agree to the extension.

No reply was received. Still waiting? Per Section §542.18, if you do not receive a response within forty (40) days from the Central Office, you are to consider this a denial at that level. Laugh or smirk here. What policy states and what actually happens are two (2) totally different things. No, you gasp, not at the BOP.

Write a letter to the Central Office Director and ask what the status of my BP-11 - Administrative Remedy Index number XXXX. I mailed it to your office on XXX XX, 2021. My BP-11 was about - use a few keywords here only—for example, missing time credit.

Wait two (2) weeks. Write the same status letter again. In your second letter, write - big and boldly - 2nd Request - HELP!! Both on the top of your letter and on the envelope in the lower right-hand corner.

The date your BP-11 was received in the Central Office was to be date-stamped onto the form and to be entered into SENTRY in the Administrative Index Log as the date received.

Once marked as received, your BP-11 will be processed. All BP-11s, whether accepted or rejected, must be entered into SENTRY at all levels and places. There is a reference manual called the Administrative Remedy Tech Reference Manual. I requested it through the Freedom of Information Act over ten (10) months ago. My reply: Due to COVID-19, there will be a short delay.

There are special rules for processing a sensitive BP-11, which is an appeal to your BP-10. It will not be logged into SENTRY until the answer or response is finished. It will also be vaguely logged in to the cloud and hide the reason it was filed to help alleviate your concerns and worries over even filing it.

BP-11s are investigated, and your reply is prepared just as your BP-9 and -10 were prepared. Notes and documents are kept in a file at the Central Office.

Was your BP-11 related to disciplinary concerns or problems? If yes, a complete set of copies is also retained with the appeal (BP-11) at the Central Office.

Once your BP-11 is completed, the Central Office will have decided on an answer to your problem or issue; an entry will be made in SENTRY, updating the index.

Finally, a copy of your appeal response will be sent to you. Your appeal will be distributed to several places. One copy will be mailed or sent to you. Another copy will be given to the Administrative Remedy Clerk or coordinator at the institution where you originally filed your BP-9 even if you have moved. A third copy will be kept in the Central Office administrative remedy file.

10

THE CLOCK IS TICKING…

REJECTED OR NO RESPONSE RECEIVED?

Waiting…waiting…still waiting…Let's discuss rejections first; then, you haven't received a response.

All rejections must have written reasons, in a notice or paper, attached to your paperwork at all levels, stating why it was rejected. There should be a Remedy ID number on the paperwork - at all levels - to verify it was even entered into SENTRY.

Does your rejection notice state a reason you can fix it and give you a time frame to correct the paperwork and resubmit it? Possible "fixable" errors commonly made include, but are not limited to, the following:

- You did not sign and/or date your BP-9, -10, or -11.

- You didn't send the required number of copies.

- You did not attach a copy of your informal resolution (8½), the previous BP-9 or BP-10 copy.

- "You must file at the institutional level. Seek your Unit Team's help." You filed your BP-9, and the institution where you are housed never responded. Per policy, no response is considered a denial, and you properly filed your BP-10 and -11. Staff at the institutional level did not correctly do their job. Your BP-9 was never entered into SENTRY.

If you received this last message, go directly to the computer. Send an electronic cop-out to the warden category. Where you would write the warden's name, write Administrative Remedy Coordinator - Urgent!! In your message, be sure and write, "Consider this an 8½!!"

Also, be sure to include the fact that you received a response to your BP-10 or BP-11 and were dismayed to discover that your BP-9 was never entered into SENTRY; nor was it given a Remedy ID number, in violation of your rights under the Administrative Remedies Program as well as a violation of your constitutional rights under both federal and state laws. Write the following in parentheses:

> "All submissions received by the Administrative Remedy Clerk or Coordinator, whether accepted or rejected, shall be entered into SENTRY."

Generally, you have five (5) days to fix or correct any defects and to resubmit your BP-9 at the institutional level, where you are housed. Usually, you will be given ten (10) days by the Regional Office to fix and/or correct defects and fifteen (15) days - calendar days - from the Central Office to fix and/or correct any defects. It should be stated in the written response they send you.

A Sensitive BP-10 rejection has special rules relating to its being rejected. The main purpose of the administrative remedy program is to solve problems and address issues that we, the unwilling residents of the BOP, bring up. Your paperwork will not be returned to you at the institution. You will receive a written notice called a rejection notice. A Remedy ID number will be noted on the rejection notice. You have the right to appeal using a BP-11.

Was your BP-10 rejected with no reasons to correct and return listed? You will need to proceed by filing a BP-11. You can appeal a rejection to the next step or level. If your BP-9 was rejected, no reasons stated, file a BP-10, and so on.

At the next level, one of three (3) things will happen. The person who receives it may agree with the rejection; secondly, the next person may say it is accepted at the regional level or at the institutional level and return it to be processed by the institution or level that rejected it; and third, the next person may accept your paperwork, file, and investigate your issue.

11

SENTRY:
ACCESS TO INDEXES AND RESPONSES & ENTRY

You, the inmate/prisoner/unwilling temporary resident of the BOP, or anyone in the free world, can ask for the Administrative Indexes and responses. Every institution at every level must make these records "available," including both the Regional and Central Offices. "Available" is the keyword here per Section §542.19 of the Administrative Remedy Program.

You must check or review the records during business hours. Copies can be purchased per the Freedom of Information Act (FOIA) fees. There is no charge per 28 C.F.R. §16.10. This information is correct as of today (April 10th, 2021) and is subject to change. Program Statement PS 1351.05 is the BOP program statement that deals with this topic and is entitled *Release of Information Program Statement.*

Records are kept for up to three (3) full years and maintained, starting with the year AFTER the case was finished.

For example, if your case status were closed in November of 1990, the records would be destroyed at the end of 1993.

The Administrative Remedy Index is to be kept on computer usage, in an accessible format, for 20 years. Pre-SENTRY Indexes also have a life span of twenty (20) years before being destroyed.

The government assigned a job number, NC1-129-83-07, to grant authority to dispose of these records, and the number is listed or provided by the National Archives.

Program Statement 5890.13. *Records Maintenance and Shredding explains* this topic in detail.

SENTRY stands for the National Online Automated Information System. SENTRY's purpose is to be the Bureau of Prisons' national online system. SENTRY is the generic name of the system; it is not an acronym. It includes most of the BOP's operation and management information needs throughout the entire BOP. It contains several specific sections, including those related to money and population management. SENTRY is to make sure there are clearly written, precise, and up-to-date instructions for every part of the BOP that SENTRY manages or keeps in the online database.

12

FREEDOM OF INFORMATION ACT (FOIA)

The Freedom of Information Act was enacted in 1966. The abbreviation is FOIA, and this act has been amended many times. The statute and laws referring to the FOIA are 28 C.F.R. 16.10 and 5 U.S.C.A. §552 (Supp 1999). The Privacy Act (PA) was established in 1974.

The Freedom of Information Act allows you to ask for and receive all types of documents that are public, especially records that relate to or are about you. Personal files that the government and other agencies maintain about you are what the Privacy Act deals with. Only you have the right to correct, change, remove, or request records that are incorrect, not complete, or do not relate to you.

You can sue in federal court if your requests are ignored or denied. We, the people, have the right to know what the government is up to. Of course, there is a catch, as always, when dealing with the government. Some records can and will be withheld if the records are in one of these categories that are allowed to be withheld. The government and its related and many agencies will make it as difficult as possible to receive the information requested.

To whom can you write and for what? That is an interesting question. The federal movement and its executive branches are what the FOIA applies to. These agencies include but are not limited to cabinet departments, the Justice Department - both the FBI and the FBOP are included here - the post office, military departments, and more. The FOIA does not cover or include the President, his staff, or offices inside the Executive Office of the President. When in doubt, write for it! You have nothing to lose but a stamp and some time.

The FOIA gives you access to any documents that are in a federal agency per 5 U.S.C.A. §552(a)(3). You may not be able to obtain all records, as some may be or are included in an exemption, which means that certain documents are not subject to the FOIA. When in doubt, write. If they write you back, saying "exempt-nope," write back stating you are appealing. You have nothing to lose and plenty to gain.

Separate laws cover state and local governments and agencies, as well as state prisons.

In federal prison, you can request access to your central file, medical records, and operational memos pursuant to §513.40 and 5 U.S.C.A.§552.28. 28 C.F.R. 513.61 relates to parts 27 through 29 of the program statement(s). You must request, in writing, access, and information in a letter to:

> Director, FBOP
> Attn: FOIA Request
> 320 First Street N.W.
> Washington, DC 20534

You must plainly print on the envelope's lower to middle left-hand side the words:

"Freedom of Information Act Request"

Do not use the abbreviation of FOIA request. Write it out. You must describe in detail the information you are seeking. Do you want this information sent to someone else? You can write in your letter that you do. Be sure to date and sign your letter in either case.

"Exceptions to Record Availability" We will now talk or write about the specific exemptions here and later in this chapter. Know that every agency has a unique list of exemptions.

The Supreme Court defined an agency record as "a document that was 1) created or obtained by an agency, and 2) is under the control of said agency at the time of the Freedom of Information Act request." This includes but is not limited to all types of forms of media - emails, papers - written, copied, typed, or faxed, faxes, photos, films, letters, computer discs, tapes or files, and audio or video recordings - that are held, owned, or stored by a government agency.

No matter what form the record is in, it is subject to being requested, and the government must try and comply with or grant your request.

You cannot write simply by asking a question. The existing agency's records must already be in that agency's possession. You must be as specific and detailed as possible in your request. The FOIA states "reasonably described." You do not have to have a document or case file number.

Your request has to have enough information and be specific enough that a government worker can locate the information without pulling out their hair in frustration. Additionally, any records requested under both the Privacy Act (PA) and the Freedom of Information Act (FOIA) must include ID and be in writing.

The power to read the contents of any record is granted to you by the Privacy Act unless a formal notice was published that a set of records is exempt from public access by law. For example, see 5. U.S.C.A §552(a), -(j), -(k).

If you are a U.S. citizen or an alien with permanent residence, you may ask for records kept in and by the federal government. You can seek records that are filed or stored by a person's name, social security number, or other identifier. Later in this chapter, I will give detailed instructions and a sample letter to use for making your request.

Exemptions to Record Availability under both the PA and the FOIA are sorted into nine (9) categories. The government uses the nine (9) categories of information that are exempt from being given out or disclosed.

However, the agency cannot say the entire file or document is exempt just because part of the file is exempt. Deletion of the part of the record that is exempt is allowed. Also, Freedom of Information Act exemptions are not mandatory. Officials have the authority to choose to waive exemptions and release information unless the information you seek is prohibited by another statute. There are nine (9) common areas that are exempt:

1. "Secret" records that are related to national security.

2. Inside every agency are internal rules for that agency; if you have a legitimate reason or a specific interest in this area, there is a limited exemption.

3. Matters exempted from disclosure, specifically by some federal statutes. For this category, there must be a specific statute that

      a) specifically states the information to be withheld, or

      b) defines and specifies the exact criteria for not giving out information.

4. Trade secrets and financial/commercial information that was given to the government to keep secret.

5. Inter-agency or intra-agency memos or letters. Suppose communication was government-to-government only, as Congress enacted. However, the government cannot use this exemption to hide facts, decisions by the agency, or policies.

6. "Medical files and personnel and similar files," which could be given to someone else, other than the person who is the subject of the file, without invading privacy. Claiming invasion of privacy is a gray area and open to interpretation. Courts give out information all the time concerning marital status, children, reputation, medical details and conditions, criminal rap sheets, and people imprisoned or incarcerated.

7. Records compiled by the police. Materials are kept by law enforcement, including the police, prosecutors, and sheriff's offices. These records consist of:

      a. Information being kept as relates to a criminal investigation;

      b. Information used for identifying individuals alleged and criminal offenders; and

      c. Reports identifiable to a person compiled at any stage of enforcement of the laws.

The CIA and the FBI try to exempt themselves totally from both the Privacy Act and the Freedom of Information Act. Nonetheless, both Acts - PA and FOIA - do cover and include both agencies, so they do fill some requests for information under both acts. You can and should request that information be released under both statutes, as both statutes do provide you with the right to access information.

Request information even if you think it is exempt. Some agencies will make information available depending on how an agency, a different office of an agency, or a court interprets the request.

A form letter received from the FBOP in response to a FOIA/PA request is included in the Appendix.

If your request is denied and an agency withholds information, you can write an appeal letter or file a lawsuit.

Here's the How-To Request Information

Every agency has set procedures that you have to follow so that your PA and FOIA request is granted. Every branch of the government may differ in its version of what constitutes a proper request under the FOIA and the PA. A list of offices you may wish to write to is included at the end of this chapter. Samples of letters I have used successfully are included in the Appendix at the end of this book.

Do you want to see your central file or medical file? Your central file is kept by the Unit Team and your Case Manager. You have the right to access it. By access, I mean viewing and making notes.

You cannot copy any pages. You must read the file in the presence of your Case Manager or other designated person, such as the Unit Team. My Case Manager gave me access without any hassle. You must request, in writing, that you wish to view your central file under both the FOIA and the PA. Allow two (2) weeks for this to occur. If not, file an 8½, your informal resolution.

Are you seeking information from the Department of Justice? The Department of Justice has a mail room and a FOIA/PA Referral Unit. Send your request to them, and the people in that office will forward your request where they feel it should go.

In writing, send your request to:

> FOIA/PA Mail Referral Unit
> U.S. Dept of Justice
> Management Division
> 950 Pennsylvania Ave N.W.
> Washington, D.C. 20530-0001

On the lower left-hand side of the envelope, write:

> "Attn: FOIA/PA Request"

Want information from the FBOP? The FBOP, or the Federal Bureau of Prisons, keeps records on past and present federal inmates, plus records relating to the administration of the FBOP.

To request records from the FBOP:

1. Your request must be in writing; and

2. Must be marked FOIA/PA Request on the envelope and in the letter; and

3. Give enough detail to let the BOP locate the records without "overworking themselves" - not having to put forth a lot of effort. (That's just a joke, right?)

You must include in the letter your full name, social security number, and place, as well as the date of birth. See the sample letters in the Appendix. You will mail your letter to:

> FOIA/PA Section
> Office of the General Counsel
> FBOP (Federal Bureau of Prisons)
> 320 First Street N.W.
> Washington, D.C. 20534

To meet the Private Act portion of your letter, you must:

1. Put your request in writing;

2. Mark it, PA Request - write FOIA/PA Request;

3. Give them as detailed or enough of an adequate idea so that the records you are requesting can be found; and

4. Verify your identity. To prove who you are, you must write your date of birth and social security number in your letter.

Before you put your letter's closing, write the following paragraph:

"I declare and certify under penalty of perjury that the foregoing is true and correct.

Dated: This the ___ day of _____, 20__."

If you don't provide details about yourself, the Department of Justice will use that as an excuse not to process your request.

The Department of Justice also has a form entitled Form DOJ-361, which they would like notarized. Since the COVID-19 pandemic, those of us in federal prison are lucky to get a cop-out or an 8½, much less this form or a notary.

Officially, the form is titled Certification of Identity. A copy of the form is shown in this book. By writing the statement found above and including your full name, citizenship status, social security number, place, and date of birth, as well as your current address, you are complying with the certification of identity request.

If you are seeking information about someone else, that person must write a statement authorizing you to receive that information. If that person is dead, you must provide proof, either an obituary or a death certificate.

Writing the FBI? To request information from the FBI, you write a letter that must include the following:

1. Letter must be written, not emailed or faxed;

2. Give your full name, date, and place of birth; and

3. Be notarized.

A note pertaining to item 3 above. Due to the difficulties in having documents notarized, counselors are giving inmates a printout of their BOP ID. Also, this printout has identifying information: name, date, place of birth, and more. The BOP, FBI, Social Security Office, and most state agencies are accepting this printout as proof of identity.

If you are seeking information about someone else and they are living, that person must give you a notarized letter stating that you can access and receive this information.

If you are asking about someone who is dead, you will need a copy of the obituary or some proof of death. A picture of the headstone at the cemetery may be acceptable. Be sure and include the cemetery's name, address, and contact information.

Costs and Fees

In your letter, you also need to say how high a "fee" you are willing to pay. If it will be more, the government is supposed to let you know the estimated cost.

Fee Waiver

You can also ask for a fee waiver. To receive a fee waiver, you must show that your request will benefit everyone, not just you. If you are indigent (broke), include that in your letter.

Send your letter to the FBI at the following address:

> FOIA/PA Request Dept.
> FBI Headquarters
> 935 Pennsylvania Ave N.W.
> Washington, D.C. 20535

Processing Your Request

The government will send you a response once it receives your request and decides on the fees. The reply will either be:

1. Your information requested; or

2. Some of your information was requested, and some of your requests were denied. The portion denied must be explained in writing; or

3. Why was your entire letter and request for information denied?

Twenty (20) business days are allowed by any agencies, including the BOP, to respond to your request. Do not count weekends or holidays. The twenty (20) days start when the BOP, or agency, receives your letter and request. An extension of time can be requested by any agency, and you will receive a form letter.

Your Request Denied?

File an administrative appeal if your request is denied. If your appeal is denied, you can file a lawsuit if you believe that the DOJ or FBOP is withholding information, that they have additional records and failed to provide them, or that the time for processing was denied. I have appealed, and surprise, surprise, I received the information - all of it - I originally requested.

Your appeal should include:

1. Write FOIA/PA Appeal on both the letter and the envelope.

2. You must submit your letter of appeal within 60 days of the notice of denial.

You mail this appeal letter to the following office:

Attn: FOIA/PA Appeal
Office of Information & Privacy
U.S. Dept. of Justice
Flag Building, Suite 570
Washington, D.C. 20530-0001

There is a number assigned to your request and the date of the letter of action. Include both in your response or appeal. There is a sample appeal letter in the appendix.

If your appeal is denied, or the agency fails to reply, you can appeal, within thirty (30) days, to:

Attorney General
Office of Information & Privacy
United States and DOJ
10th Street and Constitution Ave, N.W.
Washington, D.C. 20530

Are you considering filing a lawsuit? First, file a motion for a VAUGHN Index. The citation, or case, is found under Vaughn v. Rosen, 484 F. 2d 820 (D.C. Circuit 1973).

State FOIA Laws

Every state has a Freedom of Information Act law. Some states call these laws codes or statutes or "Ann." I do not know what "Ann" is the abbreviation for. I do not have access to this information. Unfortunately, the law library, either online or in printed books, has very limited information pertaining to state law. I have written a FOIA request to obtain this information. It is still pending.

Federal Government Agencies

Below is a list of government agencies I, or someone else, have written for. This is not a complete list of all agencies, but all I have compiled. They are in no particular order.

Internal Revenue Service (IRS)
Attn: FOIA/PA Section
111 Constitution Ave N.W.
Washington, D.C. 20224

Justice Department
FOIA/PA Section, Room 115-LOC
Justice Management Division
Washington, D.C. 20530

Note: This office will answer questions limited to which area or office to which you write and how to write your request.

Health & Human Services Dept
FOIA/PA Division
200 Independence Ave. S.W.
Room 645F, Humphrey Bldg.
Washington, D.C. 20201

Immigration & Naturalization Section (INS)
FOIA/PA Branch, 2nd Floor
ULLICO
425 I Street N.W.
Washington, D.C. 20536

Board of Immigration Appeals (BIA)
Use the above address and write on the envelope - FOIA/PA Appeal

FBI, Headquarters
935 Pennsylvania Ave. N.W.
Washington, D.C. 20535

DEA (Drug Enforcement Agency)
Attn: FOIA/PA Section
Room W-9168, LP-2
Washington, D.C. 20537

FOIA/PA Appeal
Office of Information & Privacy
U.S. Dept. of Justice
Flag Building, Suite 570
Washington, D.C. 20530-0001

*Criminal Division
Attn: FOIA/PA Division/Section
P.O. Box 65310
Washington, D.C. 20035-5310

*Civil Rights Division
Attn: FOIA/PA Division/Section
P.O. Box 65310
Washington, D.C. 20035-5310

*Please note that these last two (2) addresses were given to me. I have not written them myself.

13

EXHAUSTING YOUR REMEDIES

The Administrative Remedy Program provides every inmate with the opportunity to seek a formal review of a grievance concerning virtually any aspect of his or her confinement, should informal procedures (cop-out, informal resolution (an 8½)) not achieve a resolution. See 28 C.F.R. 542, subsection B, and Program Statement 1330.17, entitled *Administrative Remedy Program*, also 1330.18. (See page 92 to read the full program statement)

The administrative remedy program is also used to appeal an Inmate Disciplinary Sanction, commonly referred to as a "shot." You are obligated to attempt informal resolution of grievances or issues prior to filing your BP-9.

This program applies to all inmates confined in institutions by the BOP, including inmates housed at RRCS, halfway houses, and inmates whose problems occurred while imprisoned.

Sometimes, many times, courts will require you, before you file in court, to first present your problems to the BOP or to the administrative remedy process. This process is called "exhausting your remedies" by the courts. In this chapter, I will explain the various exhaustion requirements you may encounter.

A grievance procedure is supposed to meet certain statutory requirements to be acceptable. Before you sue or go to court against an agency or official, including the BOP, you are generally required to exhaust your administrative remedies. There are exemptions to the exhaustive rules. It would be futile, useless, to require exhaustion of every issue.

Yes, exhausting your remedies will defy getting your case in front of a judge. There are pros and cons to this.

Let's discuss the pros and cons of exhausting your administrative remedies.

Okay, having to exhaust your remedies will take some time (6 months to a year) and delay you from going to court. The pro is that you may get your grievance granted and win.

Many judges will dismiss your motion and write you stating that you must first exhaust your remedies. That's a con. Being able to show that you tried to resolve your issue at the prison level first may help you in court. Another pro fact is that by using the grievance system first, you may get information that will help you to succeed and win in court.

If you are considering filing a §1983 or many other motions, you must exhaust your administrative remedies first. The Prison Litigation Reform Act provides that "no civil action shall be brought by any prisoner until all administrative remedies are exhausted." 42 U.S.C. §1997 (e)(a)

If your issue or grievance occurred at the halfway house or during incarceration, this program applies. Technically, you are "in custody" until the day after you are released from supervised release, paper.

A prisoner must comply with the grievance procedures that are stated for your facility to exhaust remedies in court. *Jones v Bock*, 549 U.S. 199, 218, 127 S. Ct. 910, 166 L. Ed. 2d 798 (2007). In this case, Jones, the burden of proof was eliminated on a prisoner to prove exhaustion of administrative remedies under the Prison Litigation Reform Act. Sometimes you cannot resolve the issue and must go to court to get your jail time credits to get that detainer or warrant removed from your file. The Prison Litigation Reform Act (PLRA) has an "out," and it is dependent upon the availability and scope of the administrative remedy process.

In other words, you, the inmate, do not have to exhaust administrative remedies that *are not available, "unavailable,"* to you. There are three (3) instances when a grievance or remedy is not considered available to prisoners. These are:

1. When prison officials intimidate, play games, or don't represent, block you, the inmate, from using the grievance system; or

2. It is a dead-end as the BOP, or prison officials, are unwilling or unable to grant your grievance or give you relief or help; or

3. No ordinary prison can follow the administrative remedy process as it is so complex or convoluted, confusing, and/or

4. A threat of retaliation can also exhaust your remedies.

The courts have a two-step test to determine if an administrative remedy has been exhausted. First, the court looks at your motion to see what steps you've taken at the prison and what copies you have attached as proof. If you don't exhaust your remedies, the judge will, and often does, dismiss your motion for failure to exhaust administrative remedies. The prosecution must prove that you failed to exhaust your remedies if your motion passes the first test or phase. This is commonly called the Turner Test.

A case that discusses exceptions to exhaust your administrative remedies is *McCarthy v. Madigan*, 503 U.S. 140 (1992, Supreme Court). See also: *Washington v Barr*, No. 18-859 (2nd Cir 2019).

14

PREA AND ADMINISTRATIVE REMEDIES

The Attorney General published a rule that made national standards for preventing, detecting, reducing, and punishing prison rape. The official law is called or titled 42 U.S.C. §15607 and is published or listed in Title 28 C.F.R. §115. Here, in this book, I am only showing how a PREA, or sexual abuse administrative remedy, is handled or processed.

Before we go any further, you, who were raped or sexually abused, are not at fault. It is not your fault. Chapter 8, page 39, discusses how to file a sexual abuse or sensitive grievance. Chapter 8, pages 42-43, gives you the information on how to file an emergency and expedited grievance if you are still being assaulted and cannot get away. Email PREA or SIS for help.

There is a program statement number, PS 5342.12, entitled Sexually Abusive Behavior Prevention and Intervention Program. Section §115.52 is part of the administrative remedy program that discusses the exhaustion of administrative remedies as it relates to sexual abuse. Specifically, and I quote:

Subsection (a). "(a) an agency shall be exempt from this standard if it doesn't have administrative procedures to address grievances by inmates regarding sexual abuse."

The federal prison system does have a grievance system, so section §115.52(a) doesn't apply if you are in federal prison. However, section §115.52(b) through §115.52(g) does apply if you have a sexual abuse grievance or issue. There is no time limit on filing a BP-9 for sexual abuse. You don't have to start with an 8½. You can file an emergency and expedited grievance, as discussed in detail in Chapter 8, pages 42-43, or file a sensitive 10, as discussed in Chapter 8, page 39.

I cannot say it enough. Getting abused or raped is not your fault! On the phone booth in federal prison are red signs in both English and Spanish. The sign says:

Supportive Services for Victims of Sexual Abuse
Rape Crisis & Victim Services
(850) 681-2111
(24-hour access)

Email SIS and PREA. Your emails to both those departments will not show up in your email log under requests to staff.

APPENDIX

The following pages contain the forms in order of usage.

1. Inmate Request to Staff (cop-out)
2. Informal Resolution Process
   a) front
   b) back
3. BP-9: Request of Administrative Remedy: 1st step - at any institutional level
4. BP-10: Regional Administrative Appeal: 2nd step - at regional level
5. BP-11: Central Office Administrative Remedy Appeal - 3rd step - filed in Central Office

BP-A0148   **INMATE REQUEST TO STAFF** CDFRM
   10

U.S. DEPARTMENT OF JUSTICE   **FEDERAL BUREAU OF PRISONS**

TO:(Name and Title of Staff Member)	DATE:
FROM:	REGISTER NO.:
WORK ASSIGNMENT:	UNIT:

SUBJECT: (Briefly state your question or concern and the solution you are requesting. Continue on back, if necessary. Your failure to be specific may result in no action being taken. If necessary, you will be interviewed in order to succ_sfully respond to your request.

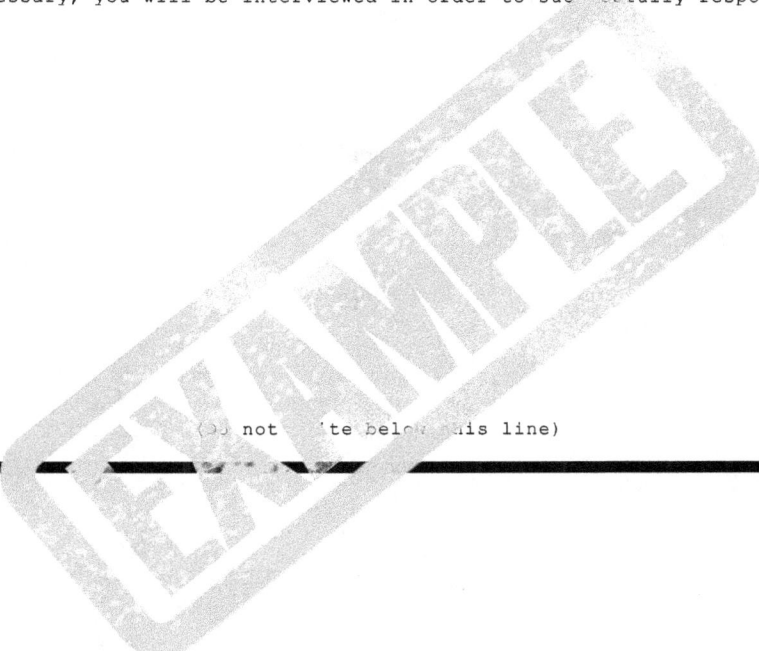

(Do not _te below _his line)

DISPOSITION:

Signature Staff Member	Date

Record Copy - File; Copy - Inmate

PDF   Prescribed by 551

This form replaces BP-148.070 dated Oct 86
and BP-S148.070 APR 94

TAL1330.13H
December 18, 2006
Page 6

Attachment A

INFORMAL RESOLUTION PROCESS

Inmate's Name and Number:_____

Date Informal Resolution Process Started:_____

Date Informal Resolution Process Concluded:_____

INFORMAL RESOLUTION PROCESS

To begin the informal resolution process, briefly state the specific complaint and your recommended resolution in Section 1. Return the form to your Correctional Counselor within two (2) working days. You and your Correctional Counselor are required to make a genuine effort at informally resolving the issue. Your Unit Manager will review the efforts at informal resolution as well. If all efforts at informal resolution fail, you will be issued a BP-9 form in which you may proceed in accordance with our policies and outlined in the institution supplement.

The informal resolution process is not in any manner, intended to prohibit you from pursuing complaints through this program. It is intended to ensure that all parties attempt to informally resolve an issue prior to initiating the formal process of filing an Administrative Remedy.

SECTION 1

Briefly state your specific complaint and recommended solution. (Please Print)

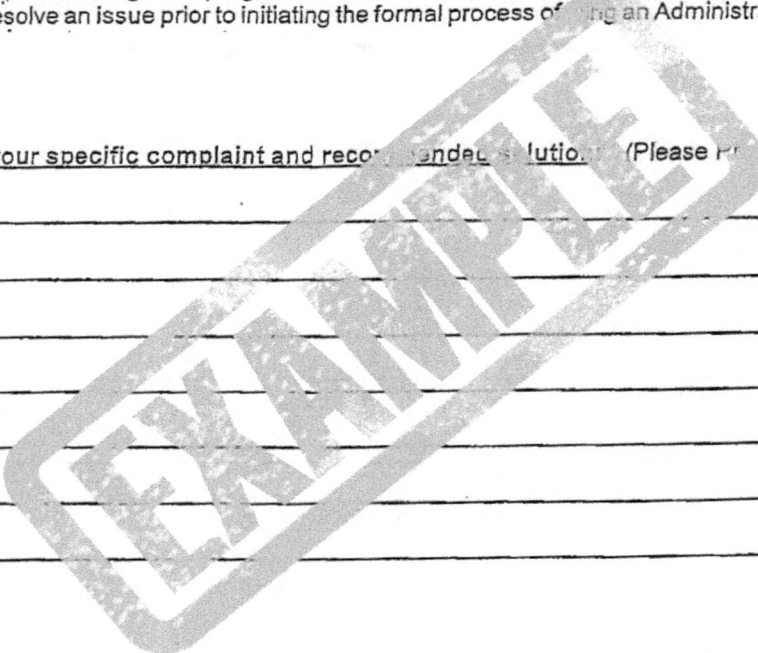

_____

_____

_____

_____

_____

_____

Administrative Remedy Instructions

- Inmate presents issue to unit counselor and requests an 8 ½.

- Inmate returns 8 ½ to unit counselor, with the front of the form completed, ensuring that the inmate name and number is on the form.

- Counselor will put the date in the "Date Informal Resolution Process Started" blank.

- Inmate allows the counselor sufficient period of time to investigate the issue and must see the counselor at a subsequent date during open house to inquire into the investigation (approximately 3 days).

- Following the discussion with the counselor about the investigation of the issue; if the issue is still not resolvable, the inmate is told to see the unit manager about the issue (1 to 2 days later).

- .Following the discussion between the inmate and the unit manager, if the issue is still not resolved, the inmate is told to see the Executive Assistant at mainline in a final attempt to resolve the issue.

- Following the discussion with the Executive Assistant, he/she will approve the unit team to issue a BP9 to the inmate. (Inmate is to see unit counselor or unit manager at open house to obtain a BP9).

- Inmate is to return the completed BP9 and any required copies to the Unit Manager or acting only for filing (the BP9 must be attached with the BP 8 ½ in order to be accepted)

- If the BP9 is submitted to anyone other than unit team, the BP9 will be rejected.

NOTE: The informal resolution process (8 ½) is a process. The inmate will not receive a written answer to the 8 ½. Additionally, inmates must complete this same process to appeal a UDC action.

U.S. DEPARTMENT OF JUSTICE

Federal Bureau of Prisons

REQUEST FOR ADMINISTRATIVE REMEDY

Type or use ball-point pen. If attachments are needed, submit four copies. Additional instructions on reverse.

From: _____

| LAST NAME, FIRST, MIDDLE INITIAL | REG. NO. | UNIT | INSTITUTION |

Part A– INMATE REQUEST

_____   _____
DATE   SIGNATURE OF REQUESTER

Part B– RESPONSE

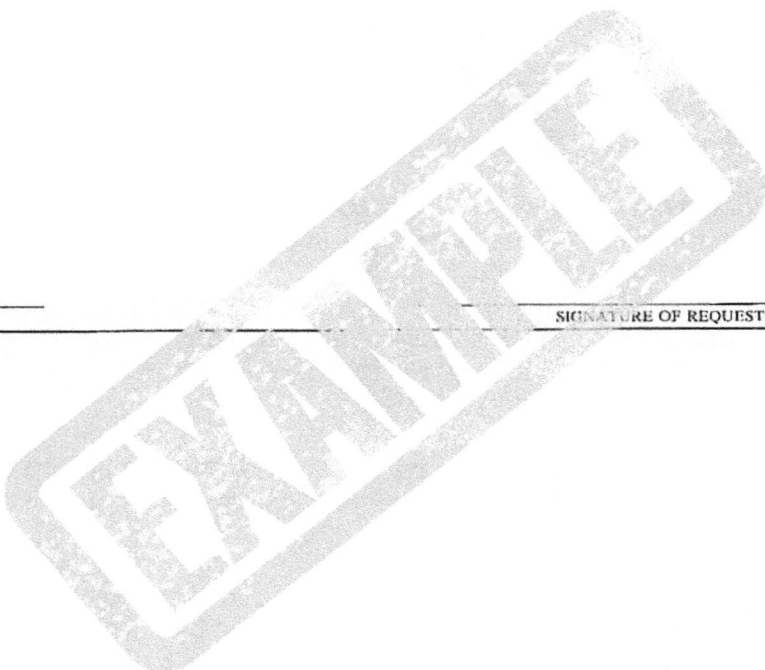

_____   _____
DATE   WARDEN OR REGIONAL DIRECTOR

If dissatisfied with this response, you may appeal to the Regional Director. Your appeal must be received in the Regional Office within 20 calendar days of the date of this response.

ORIGINAL: RETURN TO INMATE   CASE NUMBER: _____

- -
                                               CASE NUMBER: _____

Part C– RECEIPT

Return to: _____

| LAST NAME, FIRST, MIDDLE INITIAL | REG. NO. | UNIT | INSTITUTION |

SUBJECT: _____

_____   _____
DATE   RECIPIENT'S SIGNATURE (STAFF MEMBER)

USP LVN   PRINTED ON RECYCLED PAPER

BP–229(13)
APRIL 1982

U.S. Department of Justice

Federal Bureau of Prisons

Regional Administrative Remedy Appeal

Type or use ball–point pen. If attachments are needed, submit four copies. One copy of the completed BP–DIR–9 including any attachments must be submitted with this appeal.

From: _____ _____ _____ _____
            LAST NAME, FIRST, MIDDLE INITIAL   REG. NO.   UNIT   INSTITUTION

Part A—REASON FOR APPEAL

_____   _____
            DATE   SIGNATURE OF REQUESTER

Part B—RESPONSE

EXAMPLE

_____   _____
            DATE   REGIONAL DIRECTOR

If dissatisfied with this response, you may appeal to the General Counsel. Your appeal must be received in the General Counsel's Office within 30 calendar days of the date of this response.

ORIGINAL: RETURN TO INMATE   CASE NUMBER: _____

- -

Part C—RECEIPT

CASE NUMBER: _____

Return to: _____ _____ _____ _____
                LAST NAME, FIRST, MIDDLE INITIAL   REG. NO.   UNIT   INSTITUTION

SUBJECT: _____

_____   _____   BP–230(13)
USP LVN   DATE   Previous editions not usable   SIGNATURE, RECIPIENT OF REGIONAL APPEAL   APRIL 1982

U.S. Department of Justice

Central Office Administrative Remedy Appeal

Federal Bureau of Prisons

Type or use ball-point pen. If attachments are needed, submit four copies. One copy each of the completed BP-DIR-9 and BP-DIR-10, including any attachments must be submitted with this appeal.

From: _____ _____ _____ _____
       LAST NAME, FIRST, MIDDLE INITIAL   REG. NO.   UNIT   INSTITUTION

Part A—REASON FOR APPEAL

_____   _____
       DATE   SIGNATURE OF REQUESTER

Part B—RESPONSE

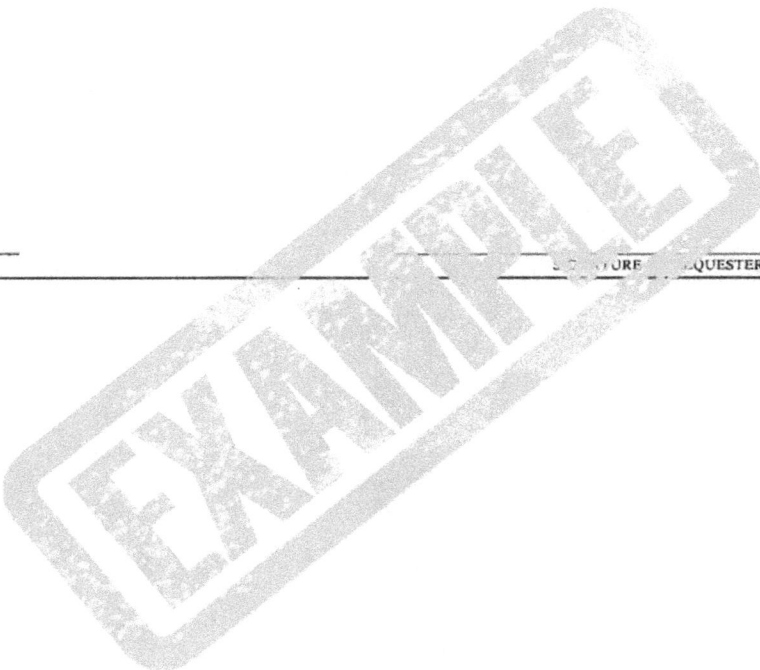

_____   _____
       DATE   GENERAL COUNSEL

ORIGINAL: RETURN TO INMATE   CASE NUMBER: _____

- -

Part C—RECEIPT

CASE NUMBER: _____

Return to: _____ _____ _____ _____
           LAST NAME, FIRST, MIDDLE INITIAL   REG. NO.   UNIT   INSTITUTION

SUBJECT: _____

_____   _____
       DATE   SIGNATURE OF RECIPIENT OF CENTRAL OFFICE APPEAL

BP-231(13)
APRIL 1982

Regional Offices

There are six Regional Offices listed in no particular order. The Central Office is the same for everyone.

Central Office
FBOP
320 First Street NW
Washington, D.C. 20534

Please note there is a director at the Central Office and each Regional Office, and you can also write. The Regional Director, Mr. Keller, with whom I spoke when he visited our facility. He followed through on looking into our issues as they relate to the COVID-19 crisis. Unfortunately, many are still not resolved.

<u>Southeast Regional Office</u>

If you are housed in Mississippi, Alabama, Georgia, South Carolina, or Puerto Rico, write this office:

Southeast Regional Office
FBOP
3800 Camp CRK PK SW/BLDG 2000
Atlanta, GA 30331

The following camps, FCIs, FCCs, and CCMs are included. I apologize if I missed one.

FCI Aliceville
FCC Yazoo City
CI Adams County
USP Atlanta
CCM Atlanta
CI McRae
CI D. Ray James
STA Glynco
FCI Jessup
FPC Montgomery
CCM Montgomery
MDC Guaynabo
FCI Bennettsville
FCI Edgefield
FCI Williamsburg
FCI Estill
FCI Miami
CCM Miami
FDC Miami
CCM Orlando
FCC Coleman
FCI Tallahassee
FPC Pensacola
FDC Tallahassee
FCI Marianna

Northeast Regional Office

Are you housed in the states of Maine, New York, Vermont, New Hampshire, Massachusetts, Connecticut, Rhode Island, New Jersey, Pennsylvania, or Ohio? The Northeast Regional's address is:

Northeast Regional Office
FBOP
2nd and Chestnut St., 7th Floor
Philadelphia, PA 19106

The following facilities are included in this region:

FCI Ray Brook

FMC Devens

FCI Danbury

FCI Otisville

FCI Fort Dix

FCI Fairton

MDC Brooklyn

CCM New York

MCC New York

FCI McKean

FCC Allenwood

USP Lewisburg

CCM Pittsburg

CCM Philadelphia

FCI Schuylkill

FCI Loretto

USP Canaan

CI Moshannon Valley

FDC Philadelphia

CI NE Ohio Correction Center

FCI Elkton

CCM Cincinnati

South Central Regional Office

Are you housed in Louisiana, Arkansas, Oklahoma, Texas, or New Mexico? This is the address of your regional office:

South Central Regional Office, FBOP
4211 Cedar Springs Rd
Dallas, TX 75219

The following institutions are included in the South Central Region:

FCC Oakdale
FCC Pollack
FCC Forest City
FTC Oklahoma City
FCC El Reno
CCM Dallas
CI Limestone
FCI Bastrop
FPC Bryan
FCC Beaumont
FDC Houston
CI Willacy County
CCM San Antonio
FCI Three Rivers
CI Eden
CI Reeves I
CI Reeves II
CI Reeves III
FCI Seagoville
FCI Ft. Worth
FMC Carswell
DC Grand Prairie
CI Big Spring
FCI Big Spring
CI Dalby
FCI Texarkana
FCI La Tuna
CI Cibola County

Western Regional Office

Are you living in one of the following states: Wyoming, Montana, Utah, Arizona, Nevada, California, Idaho, Oregon, Washington, Hawaii, or Alaska? The address you seek is:

Western Regional Office
FBOP
7338 Shoreline Drive
Stockton, CA 95219

The following facilities are included in this region:

CCM Salt Lake City

FCC Tucson

FCI Phoenix

FCI Safford

CCM Sacramento

USP Atwater

FCI Herlong

FCI Dublin

FCI Mendota

CI Taft

FCC Lompoc

MDC Los Angeles

FCI Terminal Is

CCM Long Beach

MCC San Diego

FCC Victorville

FCI Sheridan

CCM Seattle

FDC SeaTac

FDC Honolulu

Mid-Atlantic Region

Are you housed in Washington, D.C., Delaware, Maryland, Virginia, West Virginia, Kentucky, Tennessee, or North Carolina? If yes, the address to the Mid-Atlantic Regional Office is:

Mid-Atlantic Regional Office
FBOP
302 Sentinel Drive, Suite 200
Annapolis Junction, MD 20701

The following facilities or institutions are assigned to this regional office:

CCM Annapolis Junction

CCM Washington, D.C.

FCC Petersburg

USP Hazelton

FCI Morgantown

FCI Gilmer

FPC Alderson

FCI McDowell

FCI Beckley

FMC Lexington

FCI Manchester

USP Big Sandy

USP McCreary

CCM Nashville

FCI Memphis

North Central Region

Are you housed in Iowa, Illinois, Indiana, Michigan, Wisconsin, Minnesota, Missouri, North Dakota, South Dakota, Nebraska, Kansas, or Colorado? You are in the North Central Region, and the address you will write is:

North Central Regional Office
FBOP
400 State Avenue, Suite 800
Kansas City, KS 66101

The following institutions and facilities are included in the North Central Region:

MCC Chicago
FCI Pekin
FCI Greenville
USP Marion
FCC Terra Haute
FCI Milan
CCM Detroit
FCI Oxford
FPC Duluth
CCM Minneapolis
FCI Sandstone
FCI Waseca
FMC Rochester
CCM St. Louis
USMC -F -P Springfield
FPC Yankton
CCM Kansas City
UPS Leavenworth
FCI Englewood
FCC Florence
CCM Denver

Designation and Sentence Computation Center (DSCC)

The DSCC is where your timesheet, or sentence computation sheet, is calculated. Know your time was calculated incorrectly? Missing some jail credit? Skip writing R&D, who will refer you to your counselor or case manager. Write the county jail or facility where you were housed and ask for proof of incarceration. Request three (3) official copies. You will take one copy to your counselor and ask for help, stating you did not receive credit for those days. You can also send one copy with a letter to Grand Prairie, the sentence computation center's nickname.

DSCC
Grand Prairie Office Complex
U.S. Armed Forces Reserve Complex
346 Marine Forces Drive
Grand Prairie, TX 75051

Sample FOIA Letter - Version #1

Date

Freedom of Information Act/Privacy Act Section
Office of General Counsel, Room 936
320 First Street N.W.
Washington, D.C. 20534

RE: FOIA/PA Request *2nd Request*

Dear Sir or Madam/Ma'am:

This request is made pursuant to the Freedom of Information Act and the Privacy Rule. Act for the *second* time.

Documents Sought: Generalized Retrieval, otherwise known as a SENTRY print-out of all administrative remedies filed by me.

Requestor: myself - full name

Date of Birth: month, day, and year

Place of Birth: city, state

I certify that the information contained herein is true and correct.

Dated: This the _____ day of _____, 2023.

Sincerely,

Sign Your Name Here

Print Your Name Here
Fed Reg or Inmate #
FCI – Tallahassee
PO Box 5000
Tallahassee, FL 32314

Sample FOIA/PA Letter - More Formal Version #2

Date

Freedom of Information/Privacy Act Officer
Name of Agency
Address
City, State Zip Code

RE: Freedom of Information Act/Privacy Act request

Dear Sir or Madam/Ma'am:

This request is made pursuant to and under the Freedom of Information. (FOIA) and the Privacy Act, 5 U.S.C. Section §552 and 5 U.S.C. §552(a).

Please send me copies of the following documents or media: clearly list and describe the documents you are seeking and want. List dates, times if known, phone numbers, addresses, emails, cities, or states, if known, any details about the information.

As you know, the Freedom of Information Act states that if a section of a If the document is exempt from being released, the remainder of the item must be disclosed. By reason of the foregoing, I will expect to receive any and all non-. exempt parts of the records which I have requested. I also request that you justify and explain, with references to the specific exemptions of both the FOIA and the PA, any deletions not sent to me.

The information I am seeking will not be used commercially, so I don't expect to be charged fees for reviewing the materials to see if they meet or fall into one of the FOIA's or PA's exemption categories.

_____

Two choices to insert here:

Choice #1:

I agree to pay reasonable search and copy costs regarding this request. However, please notify me in advance if the total fees will be more than $___, so I can decide if it is affordable and approve the amount.

Choice #2:

The FOIA/PA provides for the waiver or reduction of search and copy fees where "the disclosure of the information is in the public interest because it is likely to significantly aid in the public's understanding of the activities or operations of the government." This request for information

is not commercial by the requester.

This request should be exempt from all fees and costs waived because (explain here how you will distribute this information received, and how those Those to whom it will be distributed will be better informed about the government's operations). If you deny this request, please notify me if the fees exceed $ so I can decide whether to appeal your decision to deny my waiver or to pay the fees.

_____

Requestor: myself - full name
Date of Birth: month, day, and year
Place of Birth: city, state

I certify that the information contained herein is true and correct.

Dated: This is the _____ day of _____ month 2023.

I certify and declare under penalty of perjury that the foregoing is true and correct.

Sincerely,

 Sign name here

Print name here
Fed Reg or Inmate #
Institution
Address
City, State Zip Code

Sample Appeal Letter

Date

Direction/Chief/Administrator
Name of Agency
Address
City, State Zip Code

Dear Director/Chief/Administrator:

This is an appeal under the Freedom of Information ACT (FOIA) 5 U.S.C. §552 and under the Privacy Act (PA) 5 U.S.C. §552(a).

On (date), I requested documents and records from your agency for (list documents & records sought). On (date), your agency denied my request because (state whatever reason the agency gave you, or no reason listed) or that the agency failed to respond within the lawful time limits. The FOIA/PA request number assigned is: _____; The Processing Office assigned is: _____.

Copies of my correspondence are attached hereto.

The requested materials are clearly able to be released under the Freedom of Information Act as well as under the Privacy Act. Your agency's policy is arbitrary, capricious, and violates my constitutional and state rights under both the Freedom of Information Act and the Privacy Act.

I have carefully reviewed 5 U.S.C. §552, 5 U.S.C. §552(a), and other legal references, including the Vaughn Index.

Please reconsider your decision to deny my request. Upon reconsideration, you will grant my request and reverse the decision to deny my request. I intend to file a lawsuit to compel disclosure if this appeal is denied.

Sincerely,

Sign name here
Print name here
Fed Reg or Inmate #
FCI – Whatever
PO Box 5XXX
City, State Zip Code

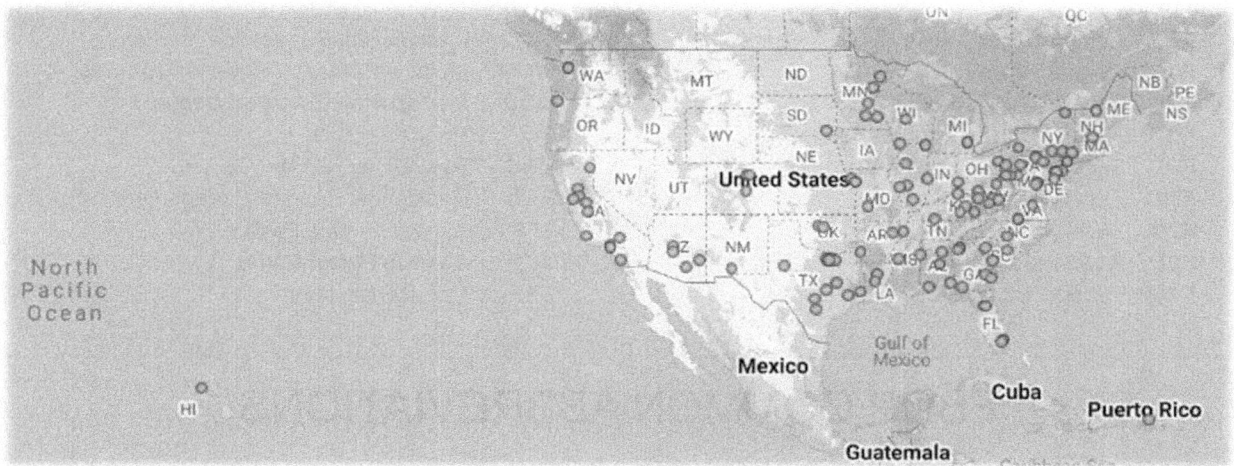

MAP OF FBOP FACILITIES: 130 FACILITIES

All Facility Types, Prison Types & Security Levels

All Prison Types

RRM - Residential Reentry Management Offices

FCC - Federal Correctional Complexes

FCI - Federal Correctional Institutions

FDC - Federal Detention Centers

FPC - Federal Prison Camps

FMC - Federal Medical Centers

FTC - Federal Transfer Centers

MCC - Metropolitan Correctional Centers

MCFP - Medical Center for Federal Prisoners

MDC - Metropolitan Detention Centers

USP - U.S. Penitentiaries

All Facility Types

Headquarters

Offices

Prisons

Training Centers

Female Facilities

All Security Levels

Minimum Security

Low Security

Medium Security

High Security

Administrative Security

ADX Administrative-Maximum U.S. Penitentiary	**MCC** Metropolitan Correctional Center
CO Central Office	**MCFP** Medical Center for Federal Prisoners
FCC Federal Correctional Complex	**MDC** Metropolitan Detention Center
FCI Federal Correctional Institution	**RO** Regional Office
FDC Federal Detention Center	**RRC** Residential Reentry Center
FMC Federal Medical Center	**RRM** Residential Reentry Management Office
FPC Federal Prison Camp	**SFF** Secure Female Facility
FSL Federal Satellite Low	**SCP** Satellite Prison Camp
FTC Federal Transfer Center	**USP** U.S. Penitentiary

FBOP COMMON ABBREVIATIONS

Central Office	North Central Region	Northeast Region	South Central Region	Southeast Region	Western Region
Central Office HQ	Chicago MCC	Allenwood FCC	Bastrop FCI	Aliceville FCI	Atwater USP
Glynco	Chicago RRM	Berlin FCI	Beaumont FCC	Atlanta RRM	Dublin FCI
Grand Prairie	Detroit RRM	Brooklyn MDC	Big Spring FCI	Atlanta USP	Herlong FCI
MSTC	Duluth FPC	Canaan USP	Bryan FPC	Bennettsville FCI	Honolulu FDC
	Englewood FCI	Cincinnati RRM	Carswell FMC	Coleman FCC	Lompoc FCC
Mid-Atlantic Region	Florence FCC	Danbury FCI	Dallas RRM	Edgefield FCI	Long Beach RRM
Alderson FPC	Greenville FCI	Devens FMC	El Reno FCI	Estill FCI	Los Angeles MDC
Ashland FCI	Kansas City RRM	Elkton FCI	Forrest City FCC	Guaynabo MDC	Mendota FCI
Baltimore RRM	Leavenworth USP	Fairton FCI	Fort Worth FMC	Jesup FCI	Phoenix FCI
Beckley FCI	Marion USP	Fort Dix FCI	Houston FDC	Marianna FCI	Phoenix RRM
Big Sandy USP	Milan FCI	Lewisburg USP	La Tuna FCI	Miami FCI	Sacramento RRM
Butner FCC	Minneapolis RRM	Loretto FCI	Oakdale FCC	Miami FDC	Safford FCI
Cumberland FCI	North Central RO	McKean FCI	Oklahoma City FTC	Miami RRM	San Diego MCC
Gilmer FCI	Oxford FCI	New York MCC	Pollock FCC	Montgomery FPC	SeaTac FDC
Hazelton FCC	Pekin FCI	New York RRM	San Antonio RRM	Montgomery RRM	Seattle RRM
Lee USP	Rochester FMC	Northeast RO	Seagoville FCI	Orlando RRM	Sheridan FCI
Lexington FMC	Sandstone FCI	Otisville FCI	South Central RO	Pensacola FPC	Terminal Island FCI
Manchester FCI	Springfield MCFP	Philadelphia FDC	Texarkana FCI	Southeast RO	Tucson FCC
McCreary USP	St Louis RRM	Philadelphia RRM	Three Rivers FCI	Talladega FCI	Victorville FCC
McDowell FCI	Terre Haute FCC	Pittsburgh RRM		Tallahassee FCI	Western RO
Memphis FCI	Thomson USP	Ray Brook FCI		Williamsburg FCI	
Mid-Atlantic RO	Waseca FCI	Schuylkill FCI		Yazoo City FCC	
Morgantown FCI	Yankton FPC				
Nashville RRM					
Petersburg FCC					
Raleigh RRM					

LIST BY REGION: FBOP FACILITIES
All Facility Types, All Prison Types & All Levels

Alabama	Florida	Kentucky	New Hampshire	South Carolina	Wisconsin
Aliceville FCI	Coleman FCC	Ashland FCI	Berlin FCI	Bennettsville FCI	Oxford FCI
Montgomery FPC	Marianna FCI	Big Sandy USP		Edgefield FCI	
Montgomery RRM	Miami FCI	Lexington FMC	New Jersey	Estill FCI	West Virginia
Talladega FCI	Miami FDC	Manchester FCI	Fairton FCI	Williamsburg FCI	Alderson FPC
	Miami RRM	McCreary USP	Fort Dix FCI		Beckley FCI
Arkansas	Orlando RRM			South Dakota	Gilmer FCI
Forrest City FCC	Pensacola FPC	Louisiana	New York	Yankton FPC	Hazelton FCC
	Tallahassee FCI	Oakdale FCC	Brooklyn MDC		McDowell FCI
Arizona		Pollock FCC	New York MCC	Tennessee	Morgantown FCI
Phoenix FCI	Georgia		New York RRM	Memphis FCI	
Phoenix RRM	Atlanta RRM	Massachusetts	Otisville FCI	Nashville RRM	
Safford FCI	Atlanta USP	Devens FMC	Ray Brook FCI		
Tucson FCC	Glynco			Texas	
	Jesup FCI	Maryland	Ohio	Bastrop FCI	
California	Southeast RO	Baltimore RRM	Cincinnati RRM	Beaumont FCC	
Atwater USP		Cumberland FCI	Elkton FCI	Big Spring FCI	
Dublin FCI	Hawaii	Mid-Atlantic RO		Bryan FPC	
Herlong FCI	Honolulu FDC		Oklahoma	Carswell FMC	
Lompoc FCC		Michigan	El Reno FCI	Dallas RRM	
Long Beach RRM	Illinois	Detroit RRM	Oklahoma City FTC	Fort Worth FMC	
Los Angeles MDC	Chicago MCC	Milan FCI		Grand Prairie	
Mendota FCI	Chicago RRM		Oregon	Houston FDC	
Sacramento RRM	Greenville FCI	Minnesota	Sheridan FCI	La Tuna FCI	
San Diego MCC	Marion USP	Duluth FPC		San Antonio RRM	
Terminal Island FCI	Pekin FCI	Minneapolis RRM	Pennsylvania	Seagoville FCI	
Victorville FCC	Thomson USP	Rochester FMC	Allenwood FCC	South Central RO	
Western RO		Sandstone FCI	Canaan USP	Texarkana FCI	
	Indiana	Waseca FCI	Lewisburg USP	Three Rivers FCI	
Colorado	Terre Haute FCC		Loretto FCI		
Englewood FCI		Missouri	McKean FCI	Virginia	
Florence FCC	Kansas	Springfield MCFP	Northeast RO	Lee USP	
MSTC	Kansas City RRM	St Louis RRM	Philadelphia FDC	Petersburg FCC	
	Leavenworth USP		Philadelphia RRM		
Connecticut	North Central RO	Mississippi	Pittsburgh RRM	Washington	
Danbury FCI		Yazoo City FCC	Schuylkill FCI	SeaTac FDC	
				Seattle RRM	
District of Columbia		North Carolina	Puerto Rico		
Central Office HQ		Butner FCC	Guaynabo MDC		
		Raleigh RRM			

LIST BY STATE: FBOP FACILITIES

All Facility Types, All Prison Types & All Levels

A	D	J	M	O	S
Alderson FPC	Dallas RRM	Jesup FCI	Manchester FCI	Oakdale FCC	Sacramento RRM
Aliceville FCI	Danbury FCI		Marianna FCI	Oklahoma City FTC	Safford FCI
Allenwood FCC	Detroit RRM	K	Marion USP	Orlando RRM	San Antonio RRM
Ashland FCI	Devens FMC	Kansas City RRM	McCreary USP	Otisville FCI	San Diego MCC
Atlanta RRM	Dublin FCI		McDowell FCI	Oxford FCI	Sandstone FCI
Atlanta USP	Duluth FPC	L	McKean FCI		Schuylkill FCI
Atwater USP		La Tuna FCI	Memphis FCI	P	Seagoville FCI
	E	Leavenworth USP	Mendota FCI	Pekin FCI	SeaTac FDC
B	Edgefield FCI	Lee USP	Miami FCI	Pensacola FPC	Seattle RRM
Baltimore RRM	El Reno FCI	Lewisburg USP	Miami FDC	Petersburg FCC	Sheridan FCI
Bastrop FCI	Elkton FCI	Lexington FMC	Miami RRM	Philadelphia FDC	South Central RO
Beaumont FCC	Englewood FCI	Lompoc FCC	Mid-Atlantic RO	Philadelphia RRM	Southeast RO
Beckley FCI	Estill FCI	Long Beach RRM	Milan FCI	Phoenix FCI	Springfield MCFP
Bennettsville FCI		Loretto FCI	Minneapolis RRM	Phoenix RRM	St Louis RRM
Berlin FCI	F	Los Angeles MDC	Montgomery FPC	Pittsburgh RRM	
Big Sandy USP	Fairton FCI		Montgomery RRM	Pollock FCC	T
Big Spring FCI	Florence FCC		Morgantown FCI		Talladega FCI
Brooklyn MDC	Forrest City FCC		MSTC	R	Tallahassee FCI
Bryan FPC	Fort Dix FCI			Raleigh RRM	Terminal Island FCI
Butner FCC	Fort Worth FMC		N	Ray Brook FCI	Terre Haute FCC
			Nashville RRM	Rochester FMC	Texarkana FCI
C	G		New York MCC		Thomson USP
Canaan USP	Gilmer FCI		New York RRM		Three Rivers FCI
Carswell FMC	Glynco		North Central RO		Tucson FCC
Central Office HQ	Grand Prairie		Northeast RO		
Chicago MCC	Greenville FCI				V
Chicago RRM	Guaynabo MDC				Victorville FCC
Cincinnati RRM					
Coleman FCC	H				W
Cumberland FCI	Hazelton FCC				Waseca FCI
	Herlong FCI				Western RO
	Honolulu FDC				Williamsburg FCI
	Houston FDC				
					Y
					Yankton FPC
					Yazoo City FCC

LIST BY ALPHA: FBOP FACILITIES

All Facility Types, All Prison Types & All Levels

FEDERAL BUREAU OF PRISONS ADDRESSES

ALDERSON FPC GLEN RAY RD. BOX A ALDERSON, WV 24910 Phone: 304-445-3300 Fax: 304-445-3320

ALICEVILLE FCI 11070 HIGHWAY 14 ALICEVILLE, AL 35442 Phone: 205-373-5000 Fax: 205-373-5020

ALLENWOOD LOW FCI RT 15, 2 MILES N OF ALLENWOOD, ALLENWOOD, PA 17810 Phone: 570-547-1990 Fax: 570-547-0343

ALLENWOOD MED FCI RT 15, 2 MI N OF ALLENWOOD WHITE DEER, PA 17810 Phone: 570-547-7950 Fax: 570-547-7751

ALLENWOOD USP RT 15, 2 MILES N OF ALLENWOOD, ALLENWOOD, PA 17810 Phone: 570-547-0963 Fax: 570-547-9201

ASHLAND FCI ST. ROUTE 716 ASHLAND, KY 41105 Phone: 606-928-6414 Fax: 606-929-4395

ATLANTA CCM 719 MCDONOUGH BLVD S.E. ATLANTA, GA 30315 Phone: 470-832-5841 Fax: 404-635-5390

ATLANTA USP 601 MCDONOUGH BLVD SE ATLANTA, GA 30315 Phone: 404-635-5100 Fax: 404-331-2403

ATWATER USP 1 FEDERAL WAY ATWATER, CA 95301 Phone: 209-386-0257 Fax: 209-386-4635

BALTIMORE CCM 400 FIRST STREET, NW 5TH FLOOR WASHINGTON, DC 20534 Phone: 202-514-8304

BASTROP FCI 1341 HIGHWAY 95 NORTH BASTROP, TX 78602 Phone: 512-321-3903 Fax: 512-304-0117

BEAUMONT LOW FCI 5560 KNAUTH ROAD BEAUMONT, TX 77705 Phone: 409-727-8172 Fax: 409-626-3500

BEAUMONT MED FCI 5830 KNAUTH ROAD BEAUMONT, TX 77705 Phone: 409-727-0101 Fax: 409-720-5000

BEAUMONT USP 6200 KNAUTH ROAD BEAUMONT, TX 77705 Phone: 409-727-8188 Fax: 409-626-3700

BECKLEY FCI 1600 INDUSTRIAL ROAD BEAVER, WV 25813 Phone: 304-252-9758 Fax: 304-256-4956

BENNETTSVILLE FCI 696 MUCKERMAN ROAD BENNETTSVILLE, SC 29512 Phone: 843-454-8200 Fax: 843-454-8219

BERLIN FCI 1 SUCCESS LOOP ROAD BERLIN, NH 03570 Phone: 603-342-4000 Fax: 603-342-4250

BIG SANDY USP 1197 AIRPORT ROAD INEZ, KY 41224 Phone: 606-433-2400 Fax: 606-433-2577

BIG SPRING FCI 1900 SIMLER AVE BIG SPRING, TX 79720 Phone: 432-466-2300 Fax: 432-466-2576

BROOKLYN MDC 80 29TH STREET BROOKLYN, NY 11232 Phone: 718-840-4200 Fax: 718-840-5005

BRYAN FPC 1100 URSULINE AVENUE BRYAN, TX 77803 Phone: 979-823-1879 Fax: 979-821-3316

BUTNER FMC OLD N. CAROLINA HWY 75 BUTNER, NC 27509 Phone: 919-575-3900 Fax: 919-575-4801

BUTNER LOW FCI OLD NC HWY 75 BUTNER, NC 27509 Phone: 919-575-5000 Fax: 919-575-5023

BUTNER MED I FCI OLD NC HWY 75 BUTNER, NC 27509 Phone: 919-575-4541 Fax: 919-575-2091

BUTNER MED II FCI OLD NC HWY 75 BUTNER, NC 27509 Phone: 919-575-8000 Fax: 919-575-8020

CANAAN USP 3057 ERIC J. WILLIAMS MEMORIAL DRIVE WAYMART, PA 18472 Phone: 570-488-8000 Fax: 570-488-8130

CARSWELL FMC NAVAL AIR STATION J ST BLDG 3000 FORT WORTH, TX 76127 Phone: 817-782-4000 Fax: 817-782-4875

CENTRAL OFFICE 320 FIRST STREET, NW WASHINGTON, DC 20534 Phone: 202-307-3198 Fax: 202-514-6620

CHICAGO CCM 1901 BUTTERFIELD ROAD, SUITE 130 DOWNERS GROVE, IL 60515 Phone: 331-903-4043 Fax: 630-271-8676

CHICAGO MCC 71 WEST VAN BUREN STREET CHICAGO, IL 60605 Phone: 312-322-0567 Fax: 312-347-4012

CINCINNATI CCM 36 E. 7TH ST., SUITE 2107-A CINCINNATI, OH 45202 Phone: 513-826-9364 Fax: 513-684-2590

COLEMAN I USP 846 NE 54TH TERRACE SUMTERVILLE, FL 33521 Phone: 352-689-6000 Fax: 352-689-6012

COLEMAN II USP 846 NE 54TH TERRACE SUMTERVILLE, FL 33521 Phone: 352-689-7000 Fax: 352-689-7012

COLEMAN LOW FCI 846 NE 54TH TERRACE SUMTERVILLE, FL 33521 Phone: 352-689-4000 Fax: 352-689-4008

COLEMAN MED FCI 846 NE 54TH TERRACE SUMTERVILLE, FL 33521 Phone: 352-689-5000 Fax: 352-689-5027

CUMBERLAND FCI 14601 BURBRIDGE RD SE CUMBERLAND, MD 21502 Phone: 301-784-1000 Fax: 301-784-1008

DALLAS CCM US ARMED FORCES RESERVE CMPL 344 MARINE FORCES DR GRAND PRAIRIE, TX 75051 Phone: 972-730-8837 Fax: 972-730-8838

DANBURY FCI 33 1/2 PEMBROKE STATION ROUTE 37 DANBURY, CT 06811 Phone: 203-743-6471 Fax: 203-312-5110

DETROIT CCM 4026 E. ARKONA RD. MILAN, MI 48160 Phone: 734-439-7653 Fax: 734-439-7671

DEVENS FMC 42 PATTON ROAD AYER, MA 01432 Phone: 978-796-1000 Fax: 978-796-1118

DUBLIN FCI 5701 8TH ST - CAMP PARKS DUBLIN, CA 94568 Phone: 925-833-7500 Fax: 925-833-7599

DULUTH FPC 4464 RALSTON DRIVE DULUTH, MN 55811 Phone: 218-722-8634 Fax: 218-733-4701

EDGEFIELD FCI 501 GARY HILL ROAD EDGEFIELD, SC 29824 Phone: 803-637-1500 Fax: 803-637-9840

EL RENO FCI 4205 HIGHWAY 66 WEST EL RENO, OK 73036 Phone: 405-262-4875 Fax: 405-319-7626

ELKTON FCI 8730 SCROGGS ROAD LISBON, OH 44432 Phone: 330-420-6200 Fax: 330-420-6436

ENGLEWOOD FCI 9595 WEST QUINCY AVENUE LITTLETON, CO 80123 Phone: 303-763-4300 Fax: 303-763-2553

ESTILL FCI 100 PRISON ROAD ESTILL, SC 29918 Phone: 803-625-4607 Fax: 803-625-5635

FAIRTON FCI 655 FAIRTON-MILLVILLE ROAD FAIRTON, NJ 08320 Phone: 856-453-1177 Fax: 856-453-4015

FLORENCE ADMAX USP 5880 HWY 67 SOUTH FLORENCE, CO 81226 Phone: 719-784-9464 Fax: 719-784-5290

FLORENCE FCI 5880 HWY 67 SOUTH FLORENCE, CO 81226 Phone: 719-784-9100 Fax: 719-784-9504

FLORENCE HIGH USP 5880 HWY 67 S FLORENCE, CO 81226 Phone: 719-784-9454 Fax: 719-784-5157

FORREST CITY FCI 1400 DALE BUMPERS ROAD FORREST CITY, AR 72335 Phone: 870-630-6000 Fax: 870-494-4496

FORREST CITY MED FCI 1400 DALE BUMPERS ROAD FORREST CITY, AR 72335 Phone: 870-494-4200 Fax: 870-494-4496

FORT DIX FCI 5756 HARTFORD & POINTVILLE RD JOINT BASE MDL, NJ 08640 Phone: 609-723-1100 Fax: 609-724-7557

FORT WORTH ADMINISTRATIVE FMC 3150 HORTON ROAD FORT WORTH, TX 76119 Phone: 817-534-8400 Fax: 817-413-3350

GILMER FCI 201 FCI LANE GLENVILLE, WV 26351 Phone: 304-626-2500 Fax: 304-626-2693

GRAND PRAIRIE OFFICE COMPLEX US ARMED FORCES RESERVE CMPL 346 MARINE FORCES DR GRAND PRAIRIE, TX 75051 Phone: 972-352-4500 Fax: 972-352-4545

GREENVILLE FCI 100 U.S. HWY 40 GREENVILLE, IL 62246 Phone: 618-664-6200 Fax: 618-664-6372

GUAYNABO MDC 652 CARRETERA 28 GUAYNABO, RQ 00965 Phone: 787-749-4480 Fax: 787-775-7824

HAZELTON FCI 1640 SKY VIEW DRIVE BRUCETON MILLS, WV 26525 Phone: 304-379-1500 Fax: 304-379-1531

HAZELTON USP 1640 SKY VIEW DRIVE BRUCETON MILLS, WV 26525 Phone: 304-379-5000 Fax: 304-379-5039

HERLONG FCI 741-925 ACCESS ROAD A-25 HERLONG, CA 96113 Phone: 530-827-8000 Fax: 530-827-8024

HONOLULU FDC 351 ELLIOTT ST HONOLULU, HI 96819 Phone: 808-838-4200 Fax: 808-838-4507

HOUSTON FDC 1200 TEXAS AVENUE HOUSTON, TX 77002 Phone: 713-221-5400 Fax: 713-229-4200

JESUP FCI 2600 HIGHWAY 301 SOUTH JESUP, GA 31599 Phone: 912-427-0870 Fax: 912-427-1125

KANSAS CITY CCM 400 STATE AVE., RM 131 KANSAS CITY, KS 66101 Phone: 913-551-1117 Fax: 913-551-1120

LA TUNA FCI 8500 DONIPHAN ROAD ANTHONY, TX 79821 Phone: 915-791-9000 Fax: 915-791-9858

LEAVENWORTH USP 1300 METROPOLITAN LEAVENWORTH, KS 66048 Phone: 913-682-8700 Fax: 913-578-1010

LEE USP LEE COUNTY INDUSTRIAL PARK HICKORY FLATS ROAD PENNINGTON GAP, VA 24277 Phone: 276-546-0150 Fax: 276-546-9115

LEWISBURG USP 2400 ROBERT F. MILLER DRIVE LEWISBURG, PA 17837 Phone: 570-523-1251 Fax: 570-522-7745

LEXINGTON FMC 3301 LEESTOWN ROAD LEXINGTON, KY 40511 Phone: 859-255-6812 Fax: 859-253-8821

LOMPOC FCI 3600 GUARD ROAD LOMPOC, CA 93436 Phone: 805-736-4154 Fax: 805-736-1292

LOMPOC USP 3901 KLEIN BLVD LOMPOC, CA 93436 Phone: 805-735-2771 Fax: 805-736-1292

LONG BEACH CCM 1299 SEASIDE AVENUE SAN PEDRO, CA 90731 Phone: 310-732-5179 Fax: 310-732-5291

LORETTO FCI 772 SAINT JOSEPH ST. LORETTO, PA 15940 Phone: 814-472-4140 Fax: 814-471-1507

LOS ANGELES MDC 535 N ALAMEDA STREET LOS ANGELES, CA 90012 Phone: 213-485-0439 Fax: 213-253-9510

MANCHESTER FCI 805 FOX HOLLOW ROAD MANCHESTER, KY 40962 Phone: 606-598-1900 Fax: 606-599-4115

MARIANNA FCI 3625 FCI ROAD MARIANNA, FL 32446 Phone: 850-526-2313 Fax: 850-718-2014

MARION USP 4500 PRISON ROAD MARION, IL 62959 Phone: 618-964-1441 Fax: 618-964-2058

MCCREARY USP 330 FEDERAL WAY PINE KNOT, KY 42635 Phone: 606-354-7000 Fax: 606-354-7190

MCDOWELL FCI 101 FEDERAL DRIVE WELCH, WV 24801 Phone: 304-436-7300 Fax: 304-436-7318

MCKEAN FCI 6975 ROUTE 59 LEWIS RUN, PA 16738 Phone: 814-362-8900 Fax: 814-363-6821

MEMPHIS FCI 1101 JOHN A DENIE ROAD MEMPHIS, TN 38134 Phone: 901-372-2269 Fax: 901-384-5462

MENDOTA FCI 33500 WEST CALIFORNIA AVENUE MENDOTA, CA 93640 Phone: 559-274-4000 Fax: 559-274-4223

MIAMI CCM 401 N MIAMI AVENUE MIAMI, FL 33128 Phone: 305-982-1181 Fax: 305-536-4024

MIAMI FCI 15801 S.W. 137TH AVENUE MIAMI, FL 33177 Phone: 305-259-2100 Fax: 305-259-2160

MIAMI FDC 33 NE 4TH STREET MIAMI, FL 33132 Phone: 305-577-0010 Fax: 305-536-7368

MID-ATLANTIC REGIONAL OFFICE 302 SENTINEL DRIVE SUITE 200 ANNAPOLIS JUNCTION, MD 20701 Phone: 301-317-3100 Fax: 301-317-3119

MILAN FCI 4004 EAST ARKONA ROAD MILAN, MI 48160 Phone: 734-439-1511 Fax: 734-439-5534

MINNEAPOLIS CCM 300 SOUTH 4TH ST, SUITE 1210 MINNEAPOLIS, MN 55415 Phone: 612-332-5026 Fax: 612-332-5029

MONTGOMERY CCM MAXWELL AFB, BLDG 1209 820 WILLOW STREET MONTGOMERY, AL 36112 Phone: 334-922-6684 Fax: 334-293-2357

MONTGOMERY FPC MAXWELL AIR FORCE BASE MONTGOMERY, AL 36112 Phone: 334-293-2100 Fax: 334-293-2329

MORGANTOWN FCI 446 GREENBAG ROAD, ROUTE 857 MORGANTOWN, WV 26501 Phone: 304-296-4416 Fax: 304-284-3600

NASHVILLE CCM 701 BROADWAY ST, SUITE 124 NASHVILLE, TN 37203 Phone: 629-266-6380 Fax: 615-736-5147

NEW YORK MCC 150 PARK ROW NEW YORK, NY 10007 Phone: 646-836-6300 Fax: 646-836-7751

NORTH CENTRAL REGIONAL OFFICE 400 STATE AVENUE, SUITE 800 KANSAS CITY, KS 66101 Phone: 913-621-3939 Fax: 913-551-1175

NORTHEAST REGIONAL OFFICE U.S. CUSTOM HOUSE, 7TH FLOOR 200 CHESTNUT STREET PHILADELPHIA, PA 19106 Phone: 215-521-7301 Fax: 215-597-1893

OAKDALE I FCI 1507 EAST WHATLEY ROAD OAKDALE, LA 71463 Phone: 318-335-4070 Fax: 318-215-2688 OAKDALE II FCI 2105

EAST WHATLEY ROAD OAKDALE, LA 71463 Phone: 318-335-4466 Fax: 318-215-2185

OKLAHOMA CITY FTC 7410 S. MACARTHUR BLVD OKLAHOMA CITY, OK 73169 Phone: 405-682-4075 Fax: 405-680-4043

ORLANDO CCM 6303 COUNTY ROAD 500 WILDWOOD, FL 34785 Phone: 352-254-6140 Fax: 352-689-7396

OTISVILLE FCI TWO MILE DRIVE OTISVILLE, NY 10963 Phone: 845-386-6700 Fax: 845-386-6727

OXFORD FCI COUNTY ROAD G & ELK AVENUE OXFORD, WI 53952 Phone: 608-584-5511 Fax: 608-584-6314

PEKIN FCI 2600 S. SECOND ST. PEKIN, IL 61554 Phone: 309-346-8588 Fax: 309-477-4670 PENSACOLA FPC 110 RABY AVE PENSACOLA, FL 32509 Phone: 850-457-1911 Fax: 850-458-7291

PETERSBURG FCI 1100 RIVER ROAD HOPEWELL, VA 23860 Phone: 804-733-7881 Fax: 804-863-1510

PETERSBURG MED FCI 1060 RIVER ROAD HOPEWELL, VA 23860 Phone: 804-504-7200 Fax: 804-504-7204

PHILADELPHIA CCM 2ND & CHESTNUT ST - 7TH FL PHILADELPHIA, PA 19106 Phone: 445-201-8783 Fax: 215-521-7486

PHILADELPHIA FDC 700 ARCH STREET PHILADELPHIA, PA 19106 Phone: 215-521-4000 Fax: 215-521-7220

PHOENIX CCM 230 N FIRST AVE, SUITE 405 PHOENIX, AZ 85003 Phone: 602-333-0537 Fax: 602-514-7076

PHOENIX FCI 37900 N 45TH AVE PHOENIX, AZ 85086 Phone: 623-465-9757 Fax: 623-465-5199

PITTSBURGH CCM 1000 LIBERTY AVENUE, STE 1315 PITTSBURGH, PA 15222 Phone: 412-395-7930 Fax: 412-434-1301

POLLOCK MED FCI 1000 AIRBASE ROAD POLLOCK, LA 71467 Phone: 318-765-4400 Fax: 318-765-4476

POLLOCK USP 1000 AIRBASE ROAD POLLOCK, LA 71467 Phone: 318-561-5300 Fax: 318-561-5391

RALEIGH CCM OLD NC 75 HIGHWAY BUTNER, NC 27509 Phone: 919-575-2080 Fax: 919-575-2073 RAY BROOK FCI 128

RAY BROOK ROAD RAY BROOK, NY 12977 Phone: 518-897-4000 Fax: 518-897-4216

ROCHESTER FMC 2110 EAST CENTER STREET ROCHESTER, MN 55904 Phone: 507-287-0674 Fax: 507-424-7600

RRM NEW YORK 201 VARICK STREET ROOM 849 NEW YORK, NY 10014 Phone: 212-336-5419

SACRAMENTO CCM 501 I STREET, SUITE 9-400 SACRAMENTO, CA 95814 Phone: 916-288-4266 Fax: 916-930-2008

SAFFORD FCI 1529 WEST HIGHWAY 366 SAFFORD, AZ 85546 Phone: 928-428-6600 Fax: 928-348-1331

SAN ANTONIO CCM 727 EAST CESAR E. CHAVEZ BLV SUITE B-138 SAN ANTONIO, TX 78206 Phone: 726-224-5472 Fax: 210-472-6224

SAN DIEGO MCC 808 UNION STREET SAN DIEGO, CA 92101 Phone: 619-232-4311 Fax: 619-595-0390

SANDSTONE FCI 2300 COUNTY RD 29 SANDSTONE, MN 55072 Phone: 320-245-2262 Fax: 320-245-0385

SCHUYLKILL FCI INTERSTATE 81 & 901 W MINERSVILLE, PA 17954 Phone: 570-544-7100 Fax: 570-544-7224

SEAGOVILLE FCI 2113 NORTH HWY 175 SEAGOVILLE, TX 75159 Phone: 972-287-2911 Fax: 972-287-5466

SEATAC FDC 2425 SOUTH 200TH STREET SEATTLE, WA 98198 Phone: 206-870-5700 Fax: 206-870-5717

SEATTLE CCM 2425 SOUTH 200 ST (AT FDC) SEATTLE, WA 98198 Phone: 206-870-1011 Fax: 206-870-1012

SHERIDAN FCI 27072 BALLSTON ROAD SHERIDAN, OR 97378 Phone: 503-843-4442 Fax: 503-843-6645

SOUTH CENTRAL REGIONAL OFFICE US ARMED FORCES RESERVE CMPL 346 MARINE FORCES DR GRAND PRAIRIE, TX 75051 Phone: 972-730-8600 Fax: 972-730-8809

SOUTHEAST REGIONAL OFFICE 3800 CAMP CRK PK SW/BDG 2000 ATLANTA, GA 30331 Phone: 678-686-1200 Fax: 678-686-1229

SPRINGFIELD USMCFP 1900 W. SUNSHINE ST SPRINGFIELD, MO 65807 Phone: 417-862-7041 Fax: 417-837-1717

ST LOUIS CCM 1222 SPRUCE ST, SUITE 6.101 ST LOUIS, MO 63103 Phone: 314-410-6818 Fax: 314-539-2465

TALLADEGA FCI 565 EAST RENFROE ROAD TALLADEGA, AL 35160 Phone: 256-315-4100 Fax: 256-315-4495

TALLAHASSEE FCI 501 CAPITAL CIRCLE, NE TALLAHASSEE, FL 32301 Phone: 850-878-2173 Fax: 850-671-6105

TERMINAL ISLAND FCI 1299 SEASIDE AVENUE SAN PEDRO, CA 90731 Phone: 310-831-8961 Fax: 310-732-5325

TERRE HAUTE FCI 4200 BUREAU ROAD NORTH TERRE HAUTE, IN 47808 Phone: 812-238-1531 Fax: 812-238-3301

TERRE HAUTE USP 4700 BUREAU ROAD SOUTH TERRE HAUTE, IN 47802 Phone: 812-244-4400 Fax: 812-244-4791

TEXARKANA FCI 4001 LEOPARD DRIVE TEXARKANA, TX 75501 Phone: 903-838-4587 Fax: 903-223-4424

THOMSON ADMIN USP 1100 ONE MILE ROAD THOMSON, IL 61285 Phone: 815-259-1000 Fax: 815-259-0186

THREE RIVERS FCI US HIGHWAY 72 WEST THREE RIVERS, TX 78071 Phone: 361-786-3576 Fax: 361-786-5051

TUCSON FCI 8901 S. WILMOT ROAD TUCSON, AZ 85756 Phone: 520-574-7100 Fax: 520-663-4406

TUCSON USP 9300 SOUTH WILMOT ROAD TUCSON, AZ 85756 Phone: 520-663-5000 Fax: 520-663-5024

VICTORVILLE MED I FCI 13777 AIR EXPRESSWAY BLVD VICTORVILLE, CA 92394 Phone: 760-246-2400 Fax: 760-246-2461

VICTORVILLE MED II FCI 13777 AIR EXPRESSWAY BLVD VICTORVILLE, CA 92394 Phone: 760-530-5700 Fax: 760-530-5706

VICTORVILLE USP 13777 AIR EXPRESSWAY BLVD VICTORVILLE, CA 92394 Phone: 760-530-5000 Fax: 760-530-5103

WASECA FCI 1000 UNIVERSITY DR, SW WASECA, MN 56093 Phone: 507-835-8972 Fax: 507-837-4547

WESTERN REGIONAL OFFICE 7338 SHORELINE DRIVE STOCKTON, CA 95219 Phone: 209-956-9700 Fax: 209-956-9793

WILLIAMSBURG FCI 8301 HIGHWAY 521 SALTERS, SC 29590 Phone: 843-387-9400 Fax: 843-387-6961

YANKTON FPC 1016 DOUGLAS AVENUE YANKTON, SD 57078 Phone: 605-665-3262 Fax: 605-668-1113

YAZOO CITY FCI 2225 HALEY BARBOUR PARKWAY YAZOO CITY, MS 39194 Phone: 662-751-4800 Fax: 662-751-4958

YAZOO CITY II FCI 2225 HALEY BARBOUR PARKWAY YAZOO CITY, MS 39194 Phone: 662-716-1020 Fax: 662-716-1036

YAZOO CITY USP 2225 HALEY BARBOUR PKWY YAZOO CITY, MS 39194 Phone: 662-716-1241 Fax: 662-716-1255

U.S. Department of Justice

Federal Bureau of Prisons

PROGRAM STATEMENT.
OPI: OGC/LIT
NUMBER: 1330.18
DATE: January 6, 2014

Administrative Remedy Program

Approved: Charles E. Samuels, Jr., Director, Federal Bureau of Prisons

1. PURPOSE AND SCOPE §542.10

a. Purpose. The purpose of the Administrative Remedy Program is to allow an inmate to seek formal review of an issue relating to any aspect of his/her own confinement. An inmate may not submit a Request or Appeal on behalf of another inmate.

Inmates seeking a formal review of issues relating to sexual abuse should use the regulations promulgated by the Department of Justice under the Prison Rape Elimination Act, 42 U.S.C. § 15606, et seq. These procedures are provided in Section 16 of this Program Statement.

b. Scope. This Program applies to all inmates in institutions operated by the Bureau of Prisons, to inmates designated to contract Community Corrections Centers (CCCs) under the Bureau of Prisons' responsibility, and to former inmates for issues that arose during their confinement. This Program does not apply to inmates confined in other non-federal facilities.

The president of a recognized inmate organization may submit a request on behalf of that organization regarding an issue that specifically affects that organization.

c. Statutorily mandated Procedures. There are statutorily mandated procedures in place for Tort claims (28 CFR 543, subpart C), Inmate Accident Compensation claims (28 CFR 301), and Freedom of Information Act or Privacy Act requests (28 CFR 513, subpart D). If an inmate raises an issue in a request or appeal that cannot be resolved through the Administrative Remedy Program, the Bureau will refer the inmate to the appropriate statutorily mandated procedures.

Federal Regulations from 28 CFR are shown in this type.

Implementing instructions are shown in this type.

2. **PROGRAM OBJECTIVES.** The expected results of this program are:

■ A procedure will be available by which inmates will be able to have any issue related to their incarceration formally reviewed by high-level Bureau officials.
■ Each request, including appeals, will be responded to within the time frames allowed.
■ A record of Inmate Administrative Remedy Requests and Appeals will be maintained.
■ Bureau policies will be more correctly interpreted and applied by staff.

3. **DIRECTIVES AFFECTED**

a. **Directive Rescinded**

P1330.17   Administrative Remedy Program (8/20/2012)

b. **Directives Referenced**

P1320.06   Federal Tort Claims Act (8/1/03)
P4500.08   Trust Fund/Deposit Fund Manual
(5/4/12) P5212.07   Control Unit Programs (2/20/01)
P5214.04   HIV Positive Inmates Who Pose Danger to Others, Procedures for Handling of (2/4/98)
P5264.08   Inmate Telephone Regulations
(1/24/08) P5270.09 Inmate Discipline Program
(7/8/11)
P5324.11   Sexually Abusive Behavior Prevention and Intervention Program (12/31/13)
P5890.13   SENTRY - National On-Line Automated Information System (12/14/99)

28 CFR 301 Inmate Accident Compensation
28 CFR 16.10 Fees (for records requested pursuant to the Freedom of Information Act (FOIA))

c. Rules cited in this Program Statement are contained in 28 CFR 542.10 through 542.19; and 28 CFR Part 115 – Prison Rape Elimination Act National Standards

4. **STANDARDS REFERENCED**

■ American Correctional Association 3rd Edition Standards for Adult Correctional Institutions: 3-4236 and 3-4271
■ American Correctional Association 3rd Edition Standards for Adult Local Detention Facilities: 3-ALDF-3C-22, and 3-ALDF-3E-11 5.

5. **RESPONSIBILITY §542.11**

a. **The Community Corrections Manager (CCM), Warden, Regional Director, and General Counsel are responsible for the implementation and operation of the Administrative Remedy Program at the Community Corrections Center (CCC), institution, regional, and Central Office levels, respectively, and shall:**

(1) Establish procedures for receiving, recording, reviewing, investigating, and responding to Administrative Remedy Requests (Requests) or Appeals (Appeals) submitted by an inmate.

See Section 13 for further information on remedy processing, including the use of SENTRY.

(2)   Acknowledge receipt of a Request or Appeal by returning a receipt to the inmate.

The receipt is generated via SENTRY.

(3)   Conduct an investigation into each Request or Appeal.

(4)   Respond to and sign all Requests or Appeals filed at their levels. At the regional level, signatory authority may be delegated to the Deputy Regional Director. At the Central Office level, signatory authority may be delegated to the National Inmate Appeals Administrator. Signatory authority extends to staff designated as acting in the capacities specified in this §542.11 but may not be further delegated without the written approval of the General Counsel.

§ 542.11 refers to Section 5 of this Program Statement.

For purposes of this Program Statement, the term "institution" includes Community Corrections Centers (CCCs); the term "Warden" includes Camp Superintendents and Community Corrections Managers (CCMs) for Requests filed by CCC inmates, and the term "inmate" includes a former inmate who is entitled to use this program.

(5)   The Warden shall appoint one staff member, ordinarily above the department head level, as the Administrative Remedy Coordinator (Coordinator) and one person to serve as Administrative Remedy Clerk (Clerk). The Regional Director and the National Inmate Appeals Administrator, Office of General Counsel, shall be advised of these appointees and any subsequent changes.

To coordinate the regional office program, each Regional Director shall also appoint an Administrative Remedy Coordinator of at least the Regional Administrator level, ordinarily the Regional Counsel, and an Administrative Remedy Clerk. The National Inmate Appeals Administrator, Office of General Counsel, shall be advised of these appointees and any subsequent changes.

(6)   The Administrative Remedy Coordinator shall monitor the program's operation at the coordinator's location and shall ensure that appropriate staff (e, g., Clerk, unit staff) have the knowledge needed to operate the procedure. The coordinator is responsible for signing any rejection notices and ensuring the accuracy of SENTRY entries, e.g., abstracts, subject codes, status codes, and dates. The coordinator also shall serve as the primary point of contact for the Warden or Regional Director in discussions of Administrative Remedies appealed to higher levels.

(7)   The Administrative Remedy Clerk shall be responsible for all clerical processing of Administrative Remedies, for accurately maintaining the SENTRY index, and for generating SENTRY inmate notices.

(8)   The Unit Manager is responsible for ensuring that inmate notices (receipts, extension notices, and receipt disregard notices from institutions, regions, and the Central Office) are printed and delivered daily for inmates in their units and for deleting those notices from SENTRY promptly after delivery to the inmate. CCMs are responsible for this function for inmates under their supervision.

b.   Inmates have the responsibility to use this Program in good faith and in an honest and straightforward manner.

6. **RESERVED**

7. **INFORMAL RESOLUTION §542.13**

a.   Informal Resolution. Except as provided in §542.13(b), an inmate shall first present an issue of concern informally to staff, and staff shall attempt to informally resolve the issue before an inmate submits a Request for Administrative Remedy. Each warden shall establish procedures to allow for the informal resolution of inmate complaints.

The Warden is responsible for ensuring that effective informal resolution procedures are in place and that good faith attempts at informal resolution are made in an orderly and timely manner by both inmates and staff. These procedures may not operate to limit inmate access to the formal filing of a Request.

b.   Exceptions. Inmates in CCCs are not required to attempt informal resolution. An informal resolution attempt is not required prior to submission to the regional or Central Office as provided for in §542.14(d) of this part. An informal resolution attempt may be waived in individual cases at the Warden's or institution's Administrative Remedy Coordinator's discretion when the inmate demonstrates an acceptable reason for bypassing informal resolution.

For example, the Warden may waive informal resolution for Unit Discipline Committee (UDC) appeals or when informal resolution is deemed inappropriate due to the issue's sensitivity.

Although not mandatory, inmates may attempt informal resolution of DHO decisions. See the Program Statement **Inmate Discipline Program**.

8. **INITIAL FILING §542.14**

a.   Submission. The deadline for completion of the informal resolution and submission of a formal written Administrative Remedy Request on the appropriate form (BP-9) is 20 calendar days following the date on which the basis for the Request occurred.

In accordance with the settlement in *Washington* v. *Reno*, and for such period of time as this settlement remains in effect, the deadline for completing informal resolution and submitting a formal written Administrative Remedy Request on the appropriate form (BP-9) (BP-229), for a disputed telephone charge, credit, or telephone service problem for which the inmate requests reimbursement to his/her telephone account, is 120 days from the date of the disputed telephone charge, credit, or telephone service problem.

Administrative Remedy Requests concerning telephone issues that do not involve billing disputes or requests for refunds for telephone service problems (such as Administrative Remedy Requests concerning telephone privileges, telephone lists, or telephone access) are governed by the 20-day filing deadline.

b.   Extension. Where the inmate demonstrates a valid reason for the delay, an extension in filing time may be allowed. In general, a valid reason for delay means a situation that prevented the inmate from submitting the request within the established time frame. Valid reasons for delay include the following: an extended period in transit during which the inmate was separated from documents needed to prepare the Request or Appeal; an extended period of time during which the inmate was physically incapable of preparing a Request or Appeal; an unusually long period taken for informal resolution attempts;

indication by an inmate, verified by staff, that a response to the inmate's request for copies of dispositions requested under §542.19 of this part was delayed.

Ordinarily, the inmate should submit written verification from staff for any claimed reason for delay.

If an inmate requests an Administrative Remedy form but has not attempted informal resolution, staff should counsel the inmate that informal resolution is ordinarily required. If the inmate nevertheless refuses to present a request informally, staff should provide the form for a formal Request. Upon receipt of the inmate's submission, the coordinator shall accept the Request if, in the coordinator's discretion, informal resolution was bypassed for valid reasons or may reject it if there are no valid reasons for bypassing informal resolution.

c. Form

(1)   The inmate shall obtain the appropriate form from CCC staff or institution staff (ordinarily, the correctional counselor).

The following forms are appropriate:

- Request for Administrative Remedy, Form BP-9 (BP-229), is appropriate for filing at the institution.
- Regional Administrative Remedy Appeal, Form BP-10 (BP-230), is appropriate for submitting an appeal to the regional office.
- Central Office Administrative Remedy Appeal, Form BP-11 (BP-231), is appropriate for submitting an appeal to the Central Office.

(2)   The inmate shall place a single complaint or a reasonable number of closely related issues on the form. If the inmate includes on a single form multiple unrelated issues, the submission shall be rejected and returned without response, and the inmate shall be advised to use a separate form for each unrelated issue. For DHO and UDC appeals, each separate incident report number must be appealed on a separate form.

Placing a single issue or closely related issues on a single form facilitates indexing and promotes efficient, timely, and comprehensive attention to the issues raised.

The inmate shall complete the form with all requested identifying information and shall state the complaint in the space provided on the form. If more space is needed, the inmate may use up to one letter-size (8 1/2" by 11") continuation page.

The inmate must provide an additional copy of any continuation page. The inmate must submit one copy of the supporting exhibits. Exhibits will not be returned with the response. Because copies of exhibits must be filed for any appeal (see § 542.15 (b) (3)), the inmate is encouraged to retain a copy of all exhibits for his or her personal records.

(3)   The inmate shall date and sign the Request and submit it to the institution staff member designated to receive such Requests (ordinarily a correctional counselor). CCC inmates may mail their Requests to the CCM.

d. Exceptions to Initial Filing at Institution

(1)   Sensitive Issues. If the inmate reasonably believes the issue is sensitive and the inmate's safety or well-being would be placed in danger if the Request became known at the

institution, the inmate may submit the Request directly to the appropriate Regional Director. The inmate shall clearly mark "Sensitive" upon the Request and explain, in writing, the reason for not submitting the Request at the institution. If the Regional Administrative Remedy Coordinator agrees that the Request is sensitive, the Request shall be accepted. Otherwise, the Request will not be accepted, and the inmate shall be advised in writing of that determination without a return of the Request. The inmate may pursue the matter by submitting an Administrative Remedy Request locally to the Warden. The Warden shall allow a reasonable extension of time for such a resubmission.

(2) **DHO Appeals. DHO appeals shall be submitted initially to the Regional Director for the region where the inmate is currently located.**

See the Program Statement **Inmate Discipline Program**.

(3) **Control Unit Appeals. Appeals related to Executive Panel Reviews of Control Unit placement shall be submitted directly to the General Counsel.**

See the Program Statement **Control Unit Programs**.

(4) **Controlled Housing Status Appeals. Appeals related to the Regional Director's review of controlled housing status placement may be filed directly with the General Counsel.**

See the Program Statement **Procedures for Handling HIV-Positive Inmates Who Pose Danger to Others**.

9. APPEALS § 542.15

a. **Submission. An inmate who is not satisfied with the Warden's response may submit an Appeal on the appropriate form (BP-10) to the appropriate Regional**

Director within 20 calendar days of the date the Warden signed the response. An inmate who is not satisfied with the Regional Director's response may submit an Appeal on the appropriate form (BP-11) to the General Counsel within 30 calendar days of the date the Regional Director signed the response. When the inmate demonstrates a valid reason for the delay, these time limits may be extended. Valid reasons for delay include those situations described in §542.14(b) of this part.

Appeal to the General Counsel is the final administrative appeal.

These deadlines specify the date of the Appeal's receipt in the regional office or the Central Office. The deadlines have been deliberately made long to allow sufficient mail time. Inmates should mail their Appeals promptly after receiving a response to ensure timely receipt.
Ordinarily, the inmate must submit written verification from institution staff for any reason for delay that cannot be verified through SENTRY.

In many cases, courts require a proper Appeal to the General Counsel before an inmate may pursue the complaint in court.

b. **Form**

(1) **Appeals to the Regional Director shall be submitted on the form designed for regional**

Appeals (BP-10) and accompanied by one complete copy or duplicate original of the institution's Request and response. Appeals to the General Counsel shall be submitted on the form designed for Central Office Appeals (BP-11) and accompanied by one complete copy or duplicate original of the institution and regional filings and their responses. Appeals shall state specifically the reason for the appeal.

(2)   An inmate may not raise an Appeal issue not raised in the lower-level filings. An inmate may not combine Appeals of separate lower-level responses (different case numbers) into a single Appeal.

(3)   An inmate shall complete the appropriate form with all requested identifying information and shall state the reasons for the Appeal in the space provided on the form. If more space is needed, the inmate may use up to one letter-size (8 1/2" x 11") continuation page. The inmate shall provide two additional copies of any continuation page and exhibits with the regional Appeal and three additional copies with an Appeal to the Central Office (the inmate is also to provide copies of exhibits used at the prior level(s) of appeal). The inmate shall date and sign the Appeal and mail it to the appropriate Regional Director if a Regional Appeal or to the National Inmate Appeals Administrator, Office of General Counsel if a Central Office Appeal (see 28 CFR part 503 for addresses of the Central Office and Regional Offices).

c. **Processing**. The appropriate regional office to process the Appeal is the regional office for the institution where the inmate is confined at the time of mailing the Appeal, regardless of the institution that responded to the institution filing.

10. **ASSISTANCE §542.16**

a.   An inmate may obtain assistance from another inmate or from institution staff in preparing a Request or an Appeal. An inmate may also obtain assistance from outside sources, such as family members or attorneys. However, no person may submit a Request or Appeal on the inmate's behalf, and obtaining assistance will not be considered a valid reason for exceeding a time limit for submission unless the delay was caused by staff.

b.   Wardens shall ensure that assistance is available for inmates who are illiterate, disabled, or who are not functionally literate in English. Such assistance includes the provision of reasonable accommodation in order for an inmate with a disability to prepare and process a Request or an Appeal.

For example, Wardens must ensure that staff (ordinarily unit staff) provide assistance in the preparation or submission of an Administrative Remedy or an Appeal upon being contacted by such inmates who are experiencing a problem.

11. **RESUBMISSION §542.17**

a.   Rejections. The coordinator at any level (CCM, institution, region, Central Office) may reject and return to the inmate without response a Request or an Appeal that is written by an inmate in a manner that is obscene or abusive or does not meet any other requirement of this part.

b.   Notice. When a submission is rejected, the inmate shall be provided a written notice, signed by the Administrative Remedy Coordinator, explaining the reason for rejection. If the defect on which the rejection is based is correctable, the notice shall inform the inmate of a

reasonable time extension within which to correct the defect and resubmit the Request or Appeal.

(1) **Sensitive Submissions**. Submissions for inmate claims that are too sensitive to be made known at the institution are not to be returned to the inmate. Only a rejection notice will be provided to the inmate. However, other rejected submissions ordinarily will be returned to the inmate with the rejection notice.

(2) **Defects**. Defects such as failure to sign a submission, failure to submit the required copies of a Request, Appeal, or attachments, or failure to enclose the required single copy of lower-level submissions are examples of correctable defects.

Ordinarily, five calendar days from the date of the notice to the inmate are reasonable for resubmission at the institution level, at least ten calendar days at the CCM or regional offices, and 15 calendar days at the Central Office.

(3) **Criteria for Rejection**. When deciding whether to reject a submission, Coordinators, especially at the institutional level, should be flexible, keeping in mind that the major purposes of this Program are to solve problems and be responsive to issues inmates raise. Thus, for example, consideration should be given to accepting a Request or Appeal that raises a sensitive or problematic issue, such as medical treatment, sentence computation, or staff misconduct, even though that submission may be somewhat untimely.

c. Appeal of Rejections. When a Request or Appeal is rejected, and the inmate is not given an opportunity to correct the defect and resubmit, the inmate may appeal the rejection, including a rejection on the basis of an exception as described in §542.14 (d), to the next appeal level. The coordinator at that level may affirm the rejection, may direct that the submission be accepted at the lower level (either upon the inmate's resubmission or direct return to that lower level), or may accept the submission for filing. The inmate shall be informed of the decision by delivery of either a receipt or a rejection notice.

12. RESPONSE TIME §542.18

If accepted, a Request or Appeal is considered filed on the date it is logged into the Administrative Remedy Index as received. Once filed, the response shall be made by the Warden or CCM within 20 calendar days, by the Regional Director within 30 calendar days, and by the General Counsel within 40 calendar days. If the Request is determined to be of an emergency nature that threatens the inmate's immediate health or welfare, the Warden shall respond not later than the third calendar day after filing. If the time period for response to a Request or Appeal is insufficient to make an appropriate decision, the time for response may be extended once by 20 days at the institutional level, 30 days at the regional level, or 20 days at the Central Office level. Staff shall inform the inmate of this extension in writing. Staff shall respond in writing to all filed Requests or Appeals. If the inmate does not receive a response within the time allotted for a reply, including an extension, the inmate may consider the absence of a response to be a denial at that level.

The date a Request or an Appeal is received in the Administrative Remedy index is entered into SENTRY as the "Date Rcv" and should be the date it is first received and date-stamped in the Administrative Remedy Clerk's office. Notice of extension ordinarily is made via SENTRY notice.

13. REMEDY PROCESSING

a. **Receipt**. Upon receiving a Request or Appeal, the Administrative Remedy Clerk shall stamp the form with the date received, log it into the SENTRY index as received on that date, and write the "Remedy ID" as assigned by SENTRY on the form. Once a submission is entered into the system, any subsequent submissions or appeals of that case shall be entered into SENTRY using the same Case Number. The "Case Number" is the purely numerical part of the "Remedy ID" which precedes the hyphen and "Submission ID."

All submissions received by the Clerk, whether accepted or rejected, shall be entered into SENTRY in accordance with the SENTRY Administrative Remedy Technical Reference Manual.

Sensitive issues, when the inmate claims that his or her safety or well-being would be placed in danger if it became known at the institution that the inmate was pursuing the issue, should be withheld from logging in until answered and/or should be logged into SENTRY with sufficient vagueness as to subject code and abstract to accommodate the inmate's concerns.

A Request should be submitted and logged in at the institution where the inmate is housed at the time the inmate gives the Request to the counselor or other appropriate staff member. If the event(s) occurred at a previous institution, staff at that previous institution shall provide, promptly upon request, any investigation or other assistance needed by the institution answering the Request. If an inmate is transferred after giving the Request to a staff member, but before that Request is logged in or answered, the institution where the Request was first given to a staff member remains responsible for logging and responding to that Request.

b. **Investigation and Response Preparation**. The Clerk or Coordinator shall assign each filed Request or Appeal for investigation and response preparation. Matters in which specific staff involvement is alleged may not be investigated by either staff alleged to be involved or by staff under their supervision. Allegations of physical abuse by staff shall be referred to the Office of Internal Affairs (OIA) in accordance with procedures established for such referrals. Where appropriate, e.g., when OIA or another agency is assuming primary responsibility for investigating the allegations, the response to the Request or Appeal may be an interim response and need not be delayed pending the outcome of the other investigation.

Requests or Appeals shall be investigated thoroughly, and all relevant information developed in the investigation shall ordinarily be supported by written documents or notes of the investigator's findings. Notes should be sufficiently detailed to show the name, title, and location of the information provided, the date the information was provided, and a full description of the information provided. Such documents and notes shall be retained with the case file copy.
When deemed necessary in the investigator's discretion, the investigator may request a written statement from another staff member regarding matters raised in the Request or Appeal.
The requested staff shall provide such statements promptly. For a disciplinary Appeal, a complete copy of the appealed disciplinary action record shall be maintained with the Appeal file copy.

c. **Responses**. Responses ordinarily shall be on the form designed for that purpose and shall state the decision reached and the reasons for the decision. The first sentence or two of a response shall be a brief abstract of the inmate's Request or Appeal, from which the SENTRY abstract should be drawn. This abstract should be complete, but as brief as possible. The remainder of the response should answer completely the Request or Appeal, be accurate and factual, and contain no extraneous information. The response should be written to be released to any inmate and the general public under the Freedom of Information Act (FOIA) and the Privacy Act. Inmate names shall not be used in responses, and staff and other names may not be used unless absolutely essential.

Program Statements, Operations Memoranda, regulations, and statutes shall be referred to in responses whenever applicable, including section numbers on which the response relies.

d. **Response Time Limits**. Responses shall be made as required in Section 12 of this Program Statement.

e. **Index Completion**. When a response is completed, the Clerk shall update SENTRY in accordance with the SENTRY Administrative Remedy Manual and the instructions in Attachment A. Particular attention should be paid to updating the status date, code, and reason, and to making any changes to the subject code and abstract indicated by the coordinator or by the response drafter. The abstract shall be taken from the response's first paragraph.

Abbreviations may be liberally used, as long as they are easily understood, to allow as complete a description of the issue in the 50 characters allotted. For consistency, the Administrative Remedy Coordinator shall approve the closing entry, including the subject codes, status code, and reason, and abstract, before the closing entry is made by the Clerk.

f. **Response Distribution**. For an institution's response, one copy of the complete Request and response shall be maintained in the Warden's Administrative Remedy File together with all supporting material. Three copies shall be returned to the inmate. An inmate who subsequently appeals to the regional or Central Office shall submit one copy with each appeal.

One copy of a Regional Appeal and response shall be retained at the regional office. One copy shall be sent to the Warden at the original filing location. The remaining two copies shall be returned to the inmate; one to submit in case of a subsequent appeal to the Central Office and one to retain.

One copy of a Central Office Appeal and response will be returned to the inmate. One copy will be retained in the Central Office Administrative Remedy File, one copy will be forwarded to the regional office where the Regional Appeal was answered, and one to the Warden's Administrative Remedy File at the original filing location.

g. **File Maintenance**. The Warden's Administrative Remedy File and Administrative Remedy Files at the Regional Offices and Central Office shall be maintained in a manner that assures case files are readily accessible to respond to inquiries from Federal Bureau of Prisons staff, inmates, and the public. Institutions shall file the Regional and Central Office response copies with the inmate's institution submission copy. Regional offices shall file copies of Central Office responses with the inmate's Regional Appeal file. Each location shall maintain copies of supporting material and investigation notes with the case file.

When a Regional or Central Office Appeal was not preceded by a lower-level filing, the institution and regional copies shall be filed at the institution and region having responsibility for the inmate at the time of response.

To provide information and feedback, Wardens and Regional Directors are encouraged to route response file copies from subsequent appeal levels to the coordinator and the appropriate department head or person who investigated and drafted the response at their respective levels.

14. ACCESS TO INDEXES AND RESPONSES §542.19

Inmates and members of the public may request access to Administrative Remedy indexes and responses, for which inmate names and Register Numbers have been removed, as indicated below. Each institution shall make available its index, and the indexes of its

regional office and the Central Office. **Each regional office shall make available its index, the indexes of all institutions in its region, and the index of the Central Office. The Central Office shall make available its index and the indexes of all institutions and regional offices. Responses may be requested from the location where they are maintained and must be identified by Remedy ID number, as indicated on an index. Copies of indexes or responses may be inspected during regular office hours at the locations indicated above or may be purchased in accordance with the regular fees established for copies furnished under the Freedom of Information Act (FOIA).**

At present, fees are detailed in 28 CFR § 16.10, which specifies a charge of $.10 per page duplicated and no charge for the first 100 pages. Staff shall forward funds received for the purchase of index and response copies to the FOIA/Privacy Act Section, Office of General Counsel, Central Office.

Any location may produce its index or that of another location by making the appropriate entries on a SENTRY retrieval transaction and specifying the "SAN" (sanitized) output format.

15. RECORDS MAINTENANCE AND DISPOSAL

a. **Disposal Authority**. The authority for Administrative Remedy records disposal is the "job number" NC1-129-83-07 provided by the National Archives.

b. **Administrative Remedy Indexes**. SENTRY Administrative Remedy indexes shall be maintained in computer-accessible form for 20 years, then destroyed. Pre-SENTRY indexes shall be maintained at the site of creation for 20 years, then destroyed.

c. **Administrative Remedy Case Files**. Administrative Remedy Case Files shall be destroyed three full years after the year in which the cases were completed (i.e., response completed). For cases submitted since the implementation of the SENTRY module (July 1990), at the end of each calendar year (beginning at the end of 1993), run SENTRY index retrieval transactions to identify the lowest case number for cases answered (status = cl* and status date in the appropriate range) during the calendar year ended three years previously. Cases below that number must be destroyed. Thus, cases answered in 1990 would be destroyed at the end of 1993; cases answered in 1991 would be destroyed at the end of 1994, etc.

To identify the lowest case number for cases answered during a given year, it may be necessary to check indexes with "Date Received" in the year in question as well as those with "Date Received" in the previous year.

Cases maintained under the pre-SENTRY numbering and filing system should be destroyed according to the following schedule:

YEAR OF CASE #	DESTROY AT END OF

16. ADMINISTRATIVE REMEDY PROCEDURES UNDER THE PRISON RAPE ELIMINATION ACT (PREA)

Title 42 U.S.C. §15607 (a) required the Attorney General to publish a final rule adopting national standards for the detection, prevention, reduction, and punishment of prison rape. Title 42 USC § 15607(b) states that the national standards shall apply immediately to the Federal Bureau of

Prisons upon adoption of the final rule. The final rule is published in Title 28 C.F.R. Part 115. This section only addresses administrative remedy procedures in relation to issues of sexual abuse and shall not constitute the sole response of the agency to allegations of sexual abuse. Appropriate steps to address the safety and security of inmates shall be made in accordance with the other provisions of the PREA regulations and the Program Statement **Sexually Abusive Behavior Prevention and Intervention Program**.

§115.52 Exhaustion of administrative remedies.

(a) An agency shall be exempt from this standard if it does not have administrative procedures to address inmate grievances regarding sexual abuse.

The Federal Bureau of Prisons has an administrative remedy system, and therefore section 115.52 (a) does not apply. The following sections, 115.52 (b) through 115.52 (g), apply to inmates seeking a formal review of issues relating to sexual abuse. For any issue not specified in sections 115.52 (b) through 115.52 (g) below, the administrative remedy system outlined in Sections 1 through 15 of this Program Statement applies.

(b)(1) The agency shall not impose a time limit on when an inmate may submit a grievance regarding an allegation of sexual abuse.

"Sexual abuse" is defined for the purposes of this section in 28 C.F.R. § 115.6, as referenced in the Bureau's policy on Sexually Abusive Behavior Prevention and Intervention Program.

Administrative remedies regarding allegations of sexual abuse may be filed at any time. For all other issues, the 20-calendar-day period specified in Section 8 of this Program Statement shall be followed. Accordingly, administrative remedies regarding an allegation of sexual abuse shall not be rejected as untimely under Section 11 of this Program Statement above.

Once filed, the inmate should follow the time requirements for appeal, as stated in Section 9 of this Program Statement above.

(2) The agency may apply otherwise-applicable time limits on any portion of a grievance that does not allege an incident of sexual abuse.

If the inmate includes on a single form multiple unrelated issues, the portion of the administrative remedy regarding allegations of sexual abuse should be accepted and processed. The inmate shall be advised to use a separate form for each unrelated issue.

(3) The agency shall not require an inmate to use any informal grievance process, or to otherwise attempt to resolve with staff, an alleged incident of sexual abuse.

Inmates are not required to attempt informal resolution under Section 7 of this Program Statement, above, regarding allegations of sexual abuse.

(4) Nothing in this section shall restrict the agency's ability to defend against an inmate lawsuit on the ground that the applicable statute of limitations has expired.

(c) The agency shall ensure that

(1) an inmate who alleges sexual abuse may submit a grievance without submitting it to a staff member who is the subject of the complaint, and

(2) Such a grievance is not referred to a staff member who is the subject of the complaint.

Matters in which specific staff involvement is alleged may not be investigated by either staff alleged to be involved or by staff under their supervision. Allegations of physical abuse by staff shall be referred to the Office of Internal Affairs (OIA) in accordance with procedures established for such referrals. Where appropriate, e.g., when OIA or another agency is assuming primary responsibility for investigating the allegations, the response to the Request or Appeal may be an interim response and need not be delayed pending the outcome of the other investigation.

(d)(1) The agency shall issue a final agency decision on the merits of any portion of a grievance alleging sexual abuse within 90 days of the initial filing of the grievance.

(2) Computation of the 90-day time period shall not include time consumed by inmates during the course of an administrative appeal.

(3) The agency may claim an extension of time to respond of up to 70 days if the normal time period for response is insufficient to make an appropriate decision. The agency shall notify the inmate in writing of any such extension and provide a date by which a decision will be made.

(4) At any level of the administrative process, including the final level, if the inmate does not receive a response within the time allotted for a reply, including any properly noticed extension, the inmate may consider the absence of a response to be a denial at that level.

Time frames in this section are consistent with Section 12 of this Program Statement above.

(e)(1) Third parties, including fellow inmates, staff members, family members, attorneys, and outside advocates, shall be permitted to assist inmates in filing requests for administrative remedies relating to allegations of sexual abuse and shall also be permitted to file such requests on behalf of inmates.

(2) If a third party files such a request on behalf of an inmate, the facility may require, as a condition of processing the request, that the alleged victim agree to have the request filed on his or her behalf and may also require the alleged victim to personally pursue any subsequent steps in the administrative remedy process.

(3) If the inmate declines to have the request processed on his or her behalf, the agency shall document the inmate's decision.

This section is applicable only to allegations of sexual abuse; inmates must personally file administrative remedies relating to other issues.

The inmate's approval of the remedy filed on his or her behalf shall be documented and include the inmate's signature. An inmate's decision to decline to have the remedy processed on his or her behalf should also be documented and include the inmate's signature. The documentation should be retained in the agency's Administrative Remedy File at the appropriate level and on Sentry in accordance with Section 13 of this Program Statement.

Responses to third-party remedies should be provided to the inmate who is the subject of the remedy.

An inmate is required to personally file any subsequent appeal. However, the inmate may receive assistance in preparing the appeal in accordance with Section 10 of this Program Statement above.

(f)(1) The agency shall establish procedures for the filing of an emergency grievance where an inmate is subject to a substantial risk of imminent sexual abuse.

This section applies when an administrative remedy alleges a substantial risk of imminent sexual abuse. If a remedy meets both of these criteria, the remedy will receive expedited processing, as described below.

Section 12 of this Program Statement provides for an "emergency" administrative remedy as required by section 115.52(f). An expedited BP-9 (BP-229) response shall be provided if a remedy is determined to be of an emergency nature that threatens the inmate's immediate health or welfare. *See* 28 C.F.R. § 542.18.

The inmate shall clearly mark "Emergency" on the BP-9 (BP-229) and explain, in writing, the reason for filing as an emergency administrative remedy under this section.

If an inmate files an emergency administrative remedy with the Warden, the local Administrative Remedy Coordinator shall make a determination as to whether the remedy alleges a substantial risk of imminent sexual abuse. If the local Administrative Remedy Coordinator agrees that the administrative remedy meets the criteria for an emergency administrative remedy, the request shall be accepted and receive expedited processing as stated below.

If the remedy is rejected for failing to meet the criteria of an emergency grievance under this section, a rejection notice will be provided to the inmate, and the remedy will be processed in accordance with the usual time frames indicated above.

(2) After receiving an emergency grievance alleging an inmate is subject to a substantial risk of imminent sexual abuse, the agency shall immediately forward the grievance (or any portion thereof that alleges the substantial risk of imminent sexual abuse) to a level of review at which immediate corrective action may be taken, shall provide an initial response within 48 hours, and shall issue a final agency decision within five calendar days. The initial response and final agency decision shall document the agency's determination of whether the inmate is at substantial risk of imminent sexual abuse and the action taken in response to the emergency grievance.

If an inmate files the emergency grievance with the institution under Section 12 of this Program Statement above, alleging a substantial risk of imminent sexual abuse, an expedited BP-9 (BP-229) response shall be provided within 48 hours. Best efforts to provide BP-10 (BP-230) and BP-11 (BP-231) responses within five calendar days should also be made in accordance with the provisions on exhaustion referenced above. If the inmate does not receive a response within the time allotted for the reply, the inmate may consider the absence of a response to be a denial at that level.

Inmates may also file "sensitive" administrative remedies under Section 8 of this Program Statement above regarding allegations of sexual abuse. If an inmate reasonably believes the issue is sensitive and the inmate's safety or well-being would be placed in danger if the remedy became known at the institution, the inmate may submit the remedy directly to the appropriate Regional Director. *See* 28 C.F.R. § 542.14 (d) (1). "Sensitive" grievances should be processed in accordance with Section 8 and Section 11 of this Program Statement, and the expedited response times specified in this section do not apply.

(g) The agency may discipline an inmate for filing a grievance related to alleged sexual abuse only where the agency demonstrates that the inmate filed the grievance in bad faith.

The maintenance of an effective sexual abuse prevention policy and the general secure and orderly running of an institution require that inmates be held responsible for manipulative behavior and false allegations. Allegations of false reports will be considered by staff in accordance with the procedures and standards of the Inmate Discipline Program policy.

17. INSTITUTION SUPPLEMENT

Each Warden shall forward a copy of any Institution Supplement developed to implement this Program Statement to the Regional Administrative Remedy Coordinator and to the National Inmate Appeals Administrator in the Central Office.

Records Retention Requirements

Requirements and retention guidance for records and information applicable to this program are available in the Records and Information Disposition Schedule (RIDS) on Sallyport.

FREEBIRD PUBLISHERS

Thanks for your interest in Freebird Publishers!

We value our customers and would love to hear from you! Reviews are an important part in bringing you quality publications. We love hearing from our readers-rather it's good or bad (though we strive for the best)!

If you could take the time to review/rate any publication you've purchased with Freebird Publishers we would appreciate it!

If your loved one uses Amazon, have them post your review on the books you've read. This will help us tremendously, in providing future publications that are even more useful to our readers and growing our business.

Amazon works off of a 5 star rating system. When having your loved one rate us be sure to give them your chosen star number as well as a written review. Though written reviews aren't required, we truly appreciate hearing from you.

Sample Review Received on Inmate Shopper

poeticsunshine

★★★★★ **Truly a guide**
Reviewed in the United States on June 29, 2023
Verified Purchase

This book is a powerhouse of information. My son had to calm/ground himself to prioritize where to start.

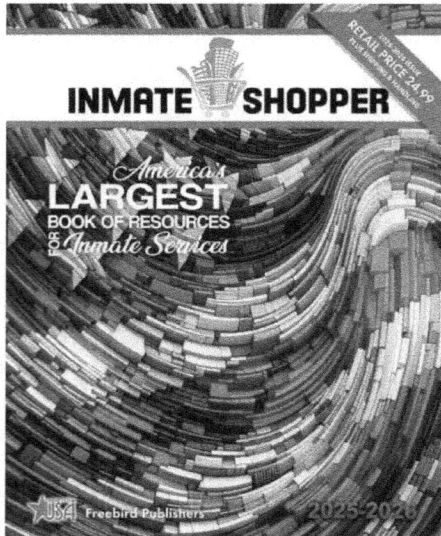

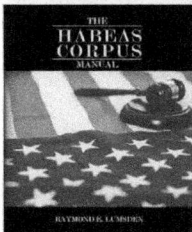

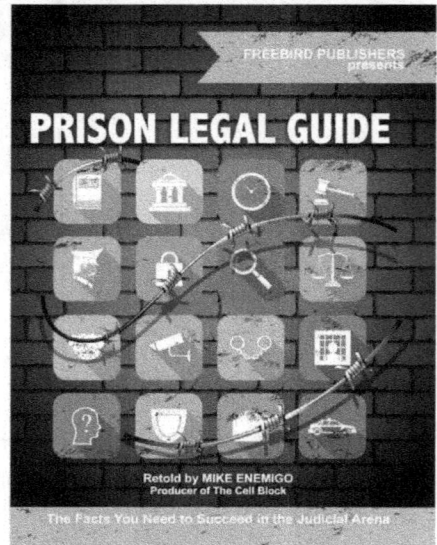

www.ingramcontent.com/pod-product-compliance
Lightning Source LLC
Chambersburg PA
CBHW081347280326
41927CB00042B/3248

9 781952 159435